DREAM LOVER

The moist darkness of the jungle night hugged me close while the murmuring drone of a thousand frogs seemed to resonate inside of me. In the black distance a flickering camp fire pulsed to the cadence of incessant drums. My feet moved in a rhythm as I found myself drawn closer and closer to the fire. Close...but hidden by the denseness of the undergrowth...I watched. Steaming sweat ran glistening off his chest, his long brown hair cast about wildly as he stomped in time with the mighty unseen drumbeats. He was alone as he danced in ecstatic fury. The sounds of the jungle throbbed in unison with this wild midnight dancer. The jungle mantra surged and contracted like a woman giving birth, in harmony with his primordial power.

Suddenly...abrupt stillness. Black stillness.

He senses that I am watching. The jungle knows that I am here. Quietly, he murmurs "Come into the light." As I step into the flickering firelight, a primal energy wells inside me. Slowly, like two shadow dancers facing each other across the fire, our bodies begin slow sensuous movements. The rhythmic humid sounds of the jungle comes to life again. The muscles of his body are fascinating. I am drawn towards his massive thighs; yet repelled by the fire's heat. Across the fire his dark, unblinking eyes follow me. His eyes, reflecting the flickering firelight, pull me like a moth to a flame as our eyes and souls connect. He steps from behind the fire. My longing becomes exhilaration as I place my hand in his.

Spinning, swirling, out of the darkness comes the light. I am consumed.

I woke from my dream feeling a mysterious inner glow. My dream lover encounter had been profound. I felt as if I had traveled back to some ancient primordial recess of myself and had embraced a wisdom born in the womb of womanhood. In the wake, I felt more womanly, fulfilled and whole. I sighed contentedly throughout the entire day as my mind returned to those intimate moments.

DREAM LOVER

DENISE LINN

The Pythagorean Press
c/o Aquarian Book Distributors Pty. Limited,
27 Power Avenue,
Alexandria NSW 2015 Australia
and

555
TRIPLE FIVE
PUBLICATIONS

Dream Lover

The Pythagorean Press
c/o Aquarian Book Distributors Pty. Limited,

27 Power Avenue, Alexandria NSW 2015 Australia and

A Triple Five Publication

A Division of Nacson and Sons Pty. Ltd
and Denise Linn Seminars
Suite 120 1463 East Republican St.
Seattle, Washington U.S.A. 98112
Telephone (206) 324 3269

First Printing - May 1990

ISBN 1 875281 00 2

Printed by Griffin Press Limited,
Marion Road, Netley, South Australia

Dedication

*To Those who enter silently in the night
and leave by dawn's light*

ACKNOWLEDGEMENTS:

Patricia Nugent, long into the night we worked, keeping our dream lovers at bay. Thank you for your unfailing support and companionship!

To Karl Bettinger, the Computer Mystic, I admire your integrity and dedication. You are a real Knight of the Light.

Barb Kelly, Medicine Woman and special friend, thank you for your perceptions!

Ann Sewell, your constant quest for excellence inspires me.

DeeAnn Grimes, Laura Melnick and Ann Street, you each have a mighty genius for expression. Thank you for editing.

Thanks to my husband David, the man of my dreams, and my daughter Meadow, my dream child.

Jenny Moalem, you are remarkable. Thank you for being who you are.

A Special Acknowledgement:

Leon Nacson, you are a noble spirit whose visions become the directions we seek.

Table of Contents

INTENT

As a new millennium beckons, we are entering into an exciting time of change and renewal in the evolutionary cycle of the planet. It is a time for the quest for inner truth. It is a time for personal evolution. There has never been a more potent time to step into the full magnificence of being human.

There are barriers to be overcome on this grand journey, however. Within the human experience, sexual inhibitions can be one of the biggest hurdles to overcome. Our sexual energy is a primary, biological driving force. When this powerful energy is blocked we are less vital and radiant. Sexual healing can be complex and it is not the intent of this book to replace in-depth counseling. The purpose of this book is to generate an honest heart space in which you can delve more deeply, into knowing the lover within. The journey has begun. May your Dream Lover help you take that first step to follow your heart, your dreams and your visions.

The dreams used in this book are real. People's names have been changed (at the request of the dreamers) with the exception of those where the real name is indicated. Some of the dreams use the exact words of the dreamers and some have been edited for easier reading.

Some of the material in *Dream Lover* was excerpted from my book *Pocketful of Dreams*. In most cases the material was revised slightly to make it appropro to Dream Lovers. For those that have read *Pocketful of Dreams*, you will find this book a handy way to review and remind yourself of familiar dream concepts, with the emphasis on obtaining a dream lover. For those readers who have not read my other books, we have attempted to make this book clear and able to stand on its own.

Excerpts from my articles *Dream Lover* and *Soulmates* from Wellbeing Magazine were used and I wish to acknowledge Barbara McGregor, publisher Wellbeing Magazine (Australia).

WHAT IS A DREAM LOVER?

A dream lover is an erotic or romantic encounter that occurs during your dreams. Your dream lover might be the type of person that you would be attracted to in waking hours or he or she might be the exact opposite of someone that you would normally find attractive. However, having dream lovers can definitely be a path to self-fulfillment. They can also provide spiritual, as well as earthy, ecstasy. They can be a way to expand love for others and self and can be used to help heal sexual difficulties. They can even be a wonderful form of evening entertainment!

My personal journey into the world of dream lovers began when I was researching the value of dreams. I ran across information indicating that active sexual activity in dreams contributed to self-actualization and confidence in waking life. Abraham Maslow, the noted American humanistic psychologist who presented the idea of self-actualization, equated potent dream lives with individuals who are self-assured, independent, composed and competent. He also stated than the dreams of a less assured person are more likely to be symbolic rather than the openly sexual dreams experienced by the person with high self-esteem.

My research in another area indicated a high correlation between sexual dreams and creativity. In one university study, the instructor of a creative writing class divided students into groups of the most creative and least creative, based upon writing assignments. The data was collected from both study groups. The non-creative students had sexually passive dreams or non-sexual dreams. The more creative students had a higher proportion of overtly sexual dreams. The researchers concluded that freedom of sexual activity in dreams is related to freedom of creative thinking.

Seeing the advantage of an active sensual dream life, and feeling that an important area of my dreams was missing, I decided to embark on gaining a dream lover. My initial attempts at creating a lover were less than the sizzling trysts I had anticipated. My first dream lover was a pale, withdrawn, insipid lad who looked about 15 years old (though he whiningly sought to convince me that he was much older). This teenager was definitely not what I had in mind. I terminated the dream.

My endeavor the following evening centered around a robust, burly man (not my type, but a definite improvement over a spindly teenage love) with a noticeable bulge in his pants. Fortunately, with my dream x-ray eyes, I could see the oversized potato he had stuck in his pants in the hope of luring me into his bed. I again made a hasty retreat.

My next attempt was a dark foreboding shadow of a presence who tried to force his attentions on me. Foiled again!

My fourth dream lover experience, finally, was more of a success. The dream was set in 18th-century Italy. This lover was neither too young nor too old. He possessed all the correct physical equipment. He was strong, kind, and romantic...he was perfect!! I even met his entire passionate, Catholic family. He then informed me we could not make love until we were married, <u>and</u> our marriage would not occur until after his older brother had married. Brother!!!

At least this gave me a clue as to why I was having so many difficulties obtaining a dream lover. My puritanical upbringing was making it unacceptable, on a subconscious level, for me to take a lover (any lover including a dream lover) in that I was already married. In discussing the situation with my husband, David, I was surprised to discover that he had always had dream lovers. He shared with me that he felt that they were important for his own sense of well being. In short he encouraged me in my nightly endeavors. I began to intensify my efforts! After a few more feeble encounters, it became <u>definitely</u> worth the effort.

Here is a letter I received from a young woman from Melbourne, Australia regarding her Dream Lover efforts.

Dear Denise,

Here are some of my dreams. My life is so enriched by my night hour experiences. I am so grateful for them.

The first dream I would like to share with you occurred after my teacher handed me your book *Pocketful of Dreams* and suggested I read the section on 'dream lovers.' Oh yes, sex and men are areas that I am working with! So that night, in bed, I read the chapter and did the visualization. I went to sleep thinking, "Oh yeah, it sounds great...BUT I can't do it!

The following dream occurred:

"I am in a beautiful bedroom, in a huge bed, everything is just perfect. With me is a man. I don't know him, but I love him. He is so kind to me, loving and gentle. We make love-slowly, softly and with an honesty I have never known. Suddenly I become aware of where I am and what I am doing. I realize that I am having a "dream lover". I am so amazed that I am able to create this experience that I wake myself up. I laugh out loud as I experience an inner warmth and glow."

Also, Denise, the next two dreams have been a source of strength for me.

August 4th, 1989

"I am on a large boat and there are many couples on board. We are in a circle and there is a man in the middle of the circle on a raised chair. His name is Jason. He is a wise man. The couples in the circle are having sex. They swap partners every so often. Jason, the Wise Man, is helping the couples in their lovemaking. As he watches us, he gives advice about how to have 'good sex'. His advice to me is that I need to change my perspective. He says I am stuck in the 'Newtonian model of sex' and I need to shift my consciousness to the 'Quantum' approach to sex. I took his advice and tried again. He stopped me again and said, "Really, Judy it is very simple. All you need to do is open your mind and experience the joy of the physical. You don't need to learn new 'sexual techniques'. You just need to change your perspective. Be more open and have less boundaries."

August 11, 1989

I meet Jason (the man from my earlier dream) at a mutual friend's house. I am surprised to see him. Our eyes meet and there is much love and friendship. We sit down in the kitchen and talk and talk. I tell him about the dream I had. We love each other. He then walks me to the car. There is a storm brewing. We stand together experiencing the electrical explosion in the sky. We don't talk. I feel so connected to the universe and Jason. The atmosphere is charged with energy. I am ALIVE.

The next day we go to the university together, each studying our separate subjects. Jason with his computers and me with my herbal medicine books. We look across at each other in the library. We are in separate worlds intellectually, but at the moment we are one.

That night we are in a lovely bedroom. There is a beautiful big bed. It is clean, fresh and inviting. Jason is lighting candles all around the room. It is beautiful. My crystals are beside the bed. We get into bed gently and softly. We cuddle together and talk softly. Our bodies melt into each other. I love Jason so deeply. I feel the love connecting me to the warmth of the sun and energy of the trees. I feel I am the universe and it is me. We are all connected and love is the life force.

Judy

WHY HAVE A DREAM LOVER?

There are many reasons to cultivate a dream lover. Perhaps one of the most important reasons is that having dream lovers can help you to become a more integrated, confident human being. Each symbol within your dream represents a part of you. Your dream is an effort to bring into harmony those different parts of yourself that are fragmented during waking life.

The word 'I' pre-supposes that each of us is a complete and whole unit. However, we are actually comprised of the most varied parts imaginable. You could almost liken each of us to a orchestra (albeit sometimes without a conductor). Periodically one or another of the "musicians" takes over and a cacophony of discordant sounds occurs as this "part" tries to dominate the other members (parts) of the orchestra.

You are like that orchestra. There will be one part of yourself that wants lose weight while there is another (subconscious) 'part' that fights to maintain the weight because that 'part' feels that the weight provides a protection or buffering from the world. There will be one part that wants to quit smoking while another part doesn't really want to stop smoking. There might be one part of you that wants to be on time and another part of you that subconsciously enjoys the excitement of the rush of the last minute. These parts can be like the orchestra that just isn't harmonizing together. It's like one part of the orchestra is playing

Pachelbel's Canon and another group is playing jazz and another whole section is asleep or dozing off. When this occurs, (when all the different parts within you are not "playing together" in unison and harmony) you feel irritation, confusion, frustration, depression, and just plain out-of-sorts.

Each part, by it's nature, is very single-minded. Each part is doing what it thinks is best for you. Never mind whether <u>you</u> like the results of that part's behavior-it will continue to "serve" you with absolute devotion. When you are displeased with what that part has created, you come down on that part with a ferocity within your internal dialogue."Why did I eat that piece of cake. I'm fat and that cake will only make me fatter!!!" The offending part will react to this abuse by redoubling it's efforts to serve you. This is because each part has received orders as to how to serve you and will steadfastly carry them out to the end. It's as if each part has its own personality and truly believes that what it is doing is in your best interest. And around and around it will go.

Sometimes an offending part will become so alienated that it seems separate from the personality. This compares to a musician who plays one tune while the conductor is directing another. The more attention he gets from the conductor, the harder he plays-only it isn't helping the music go the way the conductor would like. (Carol always has an excuse for being late. It always seems to her that something else has made her late. She feels separate from the part of herself that doesn't want to be on time.) The part that is locked out garners great energy to return to the fold and you resist even harder. This depletes some of your vital life forces. If you know someone who is always dieting you can understand this phenomenon. One part wants to lose weight, while at the same time it is at odds with the part that doesn't want to lose weight. We end up labeling some of our parts as "bad" and some as "good" and some as "completely unacceptable." It is this motley crew that dwells within you yearning for integration and unity.

Your dream lover often symbolizes a part of yourself that you are not acknowledging or owning in waking life. In a dream, sexual union can represent a coming together and a unifying of those unsyncopated parts of self. It can represent self integration. When sexual union in your dreamlife occurs, you are not suppressing or denying the part of you that your dream lover represents. You are actually embracing that part of yourself that has been denied. Thus you are becoming more whole.

Cary is an example of this. Cary was always sweet and pleasant. However, beneath the surface, a build-up of suppressed anger was festering. She was one of those individuals that never got angry and was always pleasant. This kind of individual is often a candidate for cancer and Cary was diagnosed as having pre-cancerous cells. She began to experiment with attaining a dream lover. Her first dream lover was a very angry, rebellious "James Dean" type. In her dream she felt repulsed by his angry manner and pushed him away. Continuing with her night time explorations she continued to have angry lovers but eventually she was able to move into union, and even ecstasy, with her nocturnal lovers. She quit resisting her own subconscious anger.

As a result, Cary found that she was not needing to suppress anger in her waking life. She began to communicate her needs and she began to honestly state how she felt. As she merged and found sexual union with her angry dream lovers she was able to transform, rather than suppress, the anger that was subconsciously running her. She was integrating, instead of denying her anger by uniting with the angry part of herself (represented by her dream lover). Thus she was able to have a more balanced life with the result that she was able to heal the pre-cancerous cells.

Often your dream lover will represent an aspect of yourself that you are suppressing or an attitude or ability that is latent within you. By creating a powerful union in your night hours with your dream lover you are able to integrate inner qualities and thus have a more balanced personality. It is important to acknowledge and accept ALL of your parts, even the ones that you have judged as bad or wrong.

My jungle lover allowed me to delve more deeply into my earthy nature. Rather than judge and condemn my own passionate nature, I then was able to embrace those parts of my personality. Thus I was able to love myself, all of myself, a little more.

WHY TAKE A DREAM LOVER IF YOU ARE SINGLE?

In my private practice I am often confronted by single men and women who are striving to find their soulmate or life partner. It is my observation that it is the very yearning for someone that is pushing the opportunities away. It is very difficult to pull that special individual to yourself when you are coming from neediness. The fastest way to pull the perfect partner to yourself is to feel fulfilled, whole and complete, just as you are. A dream lover can offer a single person the opportunity to feel that fulfillment.

Erotic dream work has proved useful in assisting single people to create loving relationships. Having an exciting sexual dream life can free a single person from a compulsive need to find a partner. Released from this drive, he or she can make more rational and self-loving choices about possible partners or continued celibacy.

Karyn, a 38 year old accountant,was beginning to feel desperate. She had established a success-ful, well-paying career but was feeling despon-dent without a partner. She wanted children but she didn't want to be a single mom. She felt that time was running out. She couldn't seem to help herself from wondering if every man she encoun-tered was the 'One.'

Other people sensed a neediness about Karyn. Men said that it put them off or made them uncomfortable. Karyn began to take on dream lovers. As her dream love life expanded she began to feel more whole within herself without having to be with a partner. Her dream life was satisfying an inner need. The irony is that as soon as Karyn let go of 'needing' to be in a relationship, the men "seemed to appear out of nowhere." She said, at one point, there seemed to be more men than she could handle! Karyn is now happily married and has a one year old daughter.

Here is a letter from a woman who felt that dream lovers were helping her as a single mom.

Denise,

I want to share the experiences I have had using your Dream Lover meditation. My dreams are so clear, right down to the muslin pockets on the bedspread for the fresh violets. As soon as I began to use your visualization each night, amazing things started to happen to me.

I am a single mother, with four children and I used to feel incomplete. After taking a Dream Lover my feelings of loneliness and incompleteness left me. I don't even feel alone very often. My Dream Lover always leaves dream flowers on my pillow, and when I awake in the morning I just close my eyes and know what they are.

Safe Sex

Perhaps one of the best reasons to attain a dream lover, if you are single, is because DREAM LOVERS ARE THE SAFEST SEX IN TOWN!!! In this age, too often, casual sex can end in AIDS or a sexually transmitted disease. The fear, guilt and shame that surrounds causal sex can be alleviated by taking dream lovers. This doesn't mean you need to exclude flesh and blood lovers altogether, but it does offer some viable options to the dating game.

Using Dream Lovers to Create the Perfect Lover in Waking Life

In reality, what we experience in our waking life is created by the inner thoughts and beliefs that we have. It has been said that if God came at noon and took all the money in the world, divided it, giving an equal portion to everyone, by midnight those who had been rich would be rich again and those who had been poor would be poor again. This is not just a cute story. This is close to the truth. The truth is that we tend to create for ourselves what we feel we are worth and what we deserve. In other words, we manifest our inner beliefs in our waking life. If you want to see what you believe you deserve...look at what you have. That is a sure clue.

In order to create the perfect lover, it is necessary to subconsciously believe that you deserve to be in a loving relationship. You need to be willing to release the thought that you can't find the right person. If you are continually thinking, "I would like to be in a relationship. Why can't I find someone?" Or if you are constantly wondering, "Is that him?, or "Is that her?," as you peruse a crowd, you are coming from the point of view that you are not complete because you are not in a relationship. That message is transmitted, on the inner planes, to the other people in the room and they respond by not feeling drawn to you.

In order to create a loving relationship you need to create a template or a mental image within your energy field. This mold will make it easier to manifest the relationship that you desire in conscious life. If you can create fulfilling relationships in your night hours, your brain begins to accept the reality that you do have satisfying relationships. This creates a template that can move to fruition in your waking life. Having a dream lover creates this inner thought pattern so that you can create a lover in waking life. What we believe tends to be manifested, so as you believe that you can have a loving relationship so it will be!

It works like this. Imagine that your subconscious is like a field of tall grasses. You have created a pathway through the grasses that says, "I don't have a relationship. I really want to be in a relationship that works." Henceforth, every time the idea of a relationship comes up, your mind automatically travels down the well worn path that says that you don't have a fulfilling relationship, thus reinforcing this viewpoint. Now, if in your dreams you can begin to create and experience a satisfying relationship, that well-worn path begins to grow over and a new path begins to be formed. This new path says, "I am in a fulfilling relationship." As this path becomes wider and more well-trodden, you have created a template or a mental image for a lover and a relationship. Thus, in your waking life, it is easier to pull the right relationship to yourself. This can also work in your married life. The template that you create that says, "I <u>have</u> satisfying sexual and emotional relationships," will translate to your waking life.

IS HAVING A DREAM LOVER BEING UNFAITHFUL TO YOUR PARTNER?

Often when the subject of dream lovers arises, there are concerns such as, "Am I being faithful to my husband or wife?, or "If I have night time sensual encounters will I be more likely to have an affair because I have let my guard down, so to speak?, or "Will I use up my sexual energy in my dreams and ignore my husband or wife?"

In my couple counseling, it has been my experience that taking dream lovers will <u>not</u> threaten your marriage. They, in fact, can greatly enhance your marriage. One reason men and women have affairs is because there is often the desire for something new or different or just a plain yearning for variety. If you can have experiences in your dreams that seem very life-like, not only are you able to sample the variety that you desire, but the excitement and thrill in the aftermath is transferred to your partner. If you wake up feeling more attractive-you are actually going to <u>be</u> more attractive to your mate! Try it!

Many married people have discovered that taking dream lovers allows them to satisfy urges for diversity without endangering their long-term relationship with their partner. Sara had been considering having an affair but she was terrified about the consequences for her marriage. Sara was happy in her relationship with her husband, but she wondered whether she was missing out in life because she was a virgin when she married. After taking my Dream Lover Course, Sara decided to try a dream lover instead of having an affair. Her first attempts were very rewarding and she reported intense, delicious nightly encounters. Not only did she lose her desire for an affair, but her sex life with her husband began to take on a more fulfilling dimension. Her nightly adventures added spice and excitement to her married life. Dream sex can spill over into sexual relationships between couples, adding a new spark to relationships that might have become monotonous.

CAN DREAM LOVERS MAKE YOU MORE CREATIVE?

Creativity has often been linked with the sexual force. By increasing the sexual activity in your dreams your waking creativity can increase. Jonathan was a 42 year old advertising executive from London who had reached a stagnant place in his career and life. His ideas for advertising campaigns seemed to have dried up. He said that life seemed dull and lacked luster. He had just enrolled in numerous self-help programs when he signed up for a Dream Lover Course. He said he was naturally skeptical that having dream lovers could increase his waking creativity but he felt they couldn't hurt. Although his first attempt (and even second and third) weren't Barbara Cartwright material, he finally succeeded in attaining dream lovers.

Jonathan discovered that the more successful he was in having dream lovers, the easier it was to be creative at work. Although there can be other reasons for his success at work, perhaps his ability to attain control over his dreams gave him the confidence needed to be more creative or perhaps his success was a result of the cumulative effects of all the courses together. Nevertheless his creativity did increase in direct proportion to his erotic adventures at night. He continues to enjoy nightly erotic encounters and his creativity is at a peak.

CAN DREAM LOVERS BE HEALERS?

In order to maintain a healthy body, it is imperative to have a harmonious circulation of your life force energies. When these energies are blocked, self-esteem is lowered, disease occurs and vitality diminishes. The major energy centers are called chakras.

The first chakra, the sexual center, is important to the maintenance of all the others. It is our connection to the earth. It is the home of the kundalini, that mysterious force dwelling at the base of the spine, that yogis strive to waken. It is your zest and vitality for life. Having a dream lover can assist you opening this important chakra. When this chakra opens, a woman discovers that her menstrual flow becomes easier, hormones are revitalized, her skin becomes softer, clearer and she feels rejuvenated. You have probably seen a woman who seems to be lit by her own glow. This is usually a woman whose first chakra is open and clear. The first chakra opening in a man will cause an alignment of his sexual energies and will cause him to feel more in control of his life and destiny. He also radiates a vitality and has greater clarity and certainty.

Each chakra represents a different facet of ourselves and each deserves to be developed and opened, none to the exclusion of others. However the first chakra is easily ignored by those on a spiritual path, because of guilt or denial. This area is your God-given heritage. Use it. When this chakra is open you will look healthy and be rejuvenated. As your dream lover encounters increase, your sexuality, your zest for life and your very health will increase.

I am an effective healer and have been for twenty years. When I objectively observe the energy that is flowing through me, doing my healing work, I am aware that the energy of all my chakras, including my first chakra (the sexual energy center) are activated during the healing. Now the curious phenomenon is, though I have worked on literally thousands of clients, I have yet to have any clients (to my knowledge) become sexually aroused. Yet, I hear complaints from other healers, who feel very spiritual (and don't ever experience their first chakra sexual energy activated during healing), who are dismayed to find that their clients became sexually aroused during a session. I intuit that those fulsome healers are suppressing their sexual energy, so it creates a tension that is expressed through their client. By allowing that first chakra energy to surge through the entire body, it becomes a healing energy. An additional bonus for the healer is, as that channeled energy surges from the first chakra up through all the chakras, the healer becomes healed as well.

Due to an incident as a teenager, I am minus a spleen, kidney, adrenal gland, part of a lung, part of my stomach and intestines and I have a tube out of my heart. It is my experience that it is the opening and channeling of the first chakra energy that has contributed to my own healing. Each dream lover experience will contribute to your body healing and balancing.

Mark had been suffering with a great deal of pain and discomfort for a number of years, caused by a virus which he had contracted whilst posted in Vietnam. He had undergone a variety of treatments but the pain had persisted. After attending a seminar on night healing Mark was able to report a profound dream that occurred for him. He found himself walking through an open field surrounded with deep luscious grasses. The air was hazy and he felt a soft, gentle, scented breeze brush his face. Approaching him was a woman shrouded in silk green garments. She glided towards him. He was perplexed about the situation and this woman, but he knew that he felt very sexually drawn to her. She told him to lie down and she knelt beside him. His clothes disappeared and she placed her hands over his liver area. Mark stated that he felt a very soothing warmth begin to circulate around his liver area. The warmth area became hotter and hotter until it was almost painful. When the pain became so intense that he didn't think he could take it any more, suddenly "like a balloon popping, the pain completely left", and he felt a calm peaceful feeling in his liver area.

When he awoke in the morning he said he couldn't remember when his liver area had felt so light. It has continued to feel good since that time with only the slightest twinges on a rare occasion.

Mark's experience is not unusual. Often during a healing dream there will be an intensification of pain in the affected area, followed by an abrupt cessation. To program your dream lover encounters for physical healing, see the section on programming your dreams.

CAN TAKING A DREAM LOVER CONTRIBUTE TO WORLD PEACE?

In the Far East, for thousands of years, it was thought that the underlying reality of life consisted of two dynamic energies called yin and yang. It was felt that when the forces of yin and yang were in balance, not only was the individual in harmony, but the entire world was in balance. This philosophy can explain how acquiring a dream lover can help contribute to world peace.

In Eastern Philosophy yin is the receptive feminine principle and yang is the masculine, outgoing or projecting energy. A balance of these energies is considered necessary for the harmonization of all life. Yin is embodied in the receptive energy of the moon and yang is embodied in the projecting energy of the sun. Everything is considered either yin or yang, and all of life is an interplay, a dance between these two forces. Men and women are considered the highest expression of these two powerful energies.

These two forces represent the complimentary polarities of male and female, hot and cold, day and night, sun and moon. As the *Tao Te Ching* states, "From the One came the Two, and from the Two all things were born." The pulse of life, the interplay between these two forces in the universe, affects all things. It governs the ebbing and flowing of the tides and influences the cycles within nature. In our body the tension between these two forces is symbolized by the contraction and expansion of our breath. The atoms and molecules of all things from the Great Lakes to the Great Pyramid are in constant motion, and underlying that motion is an order and a harmony. Through its vibrational nature, matter 'sings' and those songs are carried forth on waves, pulsating electron waves that become all matter. Existence is sustained by the on and off pulse, the alternating current of both forces, in perfect balance, the yin and yang, male and female, dark and light.

In ancient times there was more of a balance between these two forces than in present times. The feminine principle was as fully revered as the masculine principle. In many major archaeological finds around the world, the image of the goddess emerges again and again. She was the primary symbol for the feminine principle, the inner reality of life, made manifest in the sky, the moon, the stars, the flowing rivers, the morning dew, the fertile earth and our nightly dreams. The people of ancient cultures worshipped that symbol and they revered and understood nature. To them the invisible forces were very real, and they felt that an adherence to those inner laws that were the domain of the female (or yin force) were necessary to maintain a balance in life. Hence, through the ages, temples and shrines for initiation into the mysteries of the goddess were erected and maintained. However, with the passing of time, the temples and shrines turned to dust. The world became very outer-consciousness oriented, very left-brained. We lost sight of the guidance of the right brain and those goddess states of being such as meditation, dreams and visions-those states of being that were so important to early people.

Since the decline of the goddess religions, we have lacked the spiritual directives that teach us to honor the earth. However, the ancient feminine principle is beginning to re-assert its power- not as a religious tenet, but as an incredible inner force, rising to shape this planet's destiny.

In my training and apprenticeship with native peoples (including Native Americans, the Maoris of New Zealand and the Australian Aborigines) one theme has emerged consistently. The idea which has been reinforced is the critical need for each of us to return to the female principle, so that there might be a balance within our planet. This means that we each need to honor our intuition and our dreams, protect mother earth and cherish the inner mysteries of self. These are all part of the feminine principle.

An Australian aboriginal elder explained it to me this way. The links of the crystal energy grid that unite the earth and keep the planet in a balance, are weakening. He said this is occurring because the masculine principle within the world has contributed to a wounded planet through pollution of the water and air and the destruction of the forests and sacred sites of the world. The masculine principle includes qualities such as conquering, left-brained rational thinking and being territorial. This doesn't necessarily mean that men are responsible for the critical shape of our planet. The aborigine was referring to the masculine way of perceiving the world of which both men and women have been responsible in recent years. He stated that it is imperative to return to the feminine principle to balance the male and female energies of the planet so that there is more peace on earth.

The fastest way to contribute to a balance of the male and female energies of the planet is to create a harmony between the male and female energies that dwell within you. There are many ways to balance the inner male and female energies. Taking a Dream Lover is one way to balance both poles of duality. Your Dream Lover can allow you to develop an integration of the yin and yang attributes in your own personality. This is possible because your dream lover characteristics represent parts of yourself. From a psychological perspective, when you are making love in your dreams you are actually integrating aspects of your personality and healing the male and female energies within yourself.

For example, as a man, if you make love with a female in your dreams, you are aligning the female aspects of yourself. The female or yin aspect is symbolized by receptivity, intuition and inner life. So as you dream you are embracing the woman of your dreams, you are also embracing those qualities within yourself that are represented by the female principle. You are expanding your intuition, gentleness and inner life. The same is true if a woman dreams of making love with a man. In her midnight rendezvous she is embracing her own male aspects, such as her ability to focus and project into the world. As a result of her nightly lovemaking she will be able to be more assertive and result-oriented during waking life.

Sometimes a heterosexual man or woman will dream they are having a sexual experience with someone of their own sex. For some, this can be disturbing. However, most often this is a balancing of those male and female aspects within. A heterosexual woman dreaming of making love with a woman may bring more yin (or receptive) qualities into her life. Likewise, a heterosexual man dreaming of making love with a man may need to become more yang (or outgoing) in waking life and this may be his subconscious way of achieving this. A heterosexual man dreaming of making love to a man does not necessarily mean that he is a latent homosexual.

It can be just as disturbing for a homosexual man or woman to dream of making love to the opposite sex. This, again, does not necessarily indicate a change of sexual preference. It can be a balancing of the inner male and female energies.

CAN DREAM LOVERS HELP YOU BE-COME MORE SPIRITUALLY ATTUNED?

The pursuit of dream lovers can be a pathway to spiritual growth and evolvement. In ancient cultures, the understanding of sexuality and sensuality was considered basic to the expression of life. In the East, it was a means of expressing unity with Spirit. Sexuality was looked upon as a path to mystical experience. Sexual union was considered a way to break through the illusion of duality-a way to attain liberation and enhance health and well-being. It was felt that within each male was a latent female or yin energy and within each female was a latent male or yang energy. Sexual union was considered a way to unite these opposing, yet harmonious, forces in the universe and thus become closer with God.

In the last 20 years, sexual taboos and inhibitions have been breaking down, but unless there is a correct understanding of the use and power of sexuality, sexual liberation will contribute to feelings of emptiness, unfulfillment and lack of purpose. There is great power in the divine union of a man and a woman dedicated to the expression of their higher selves. When there is a holy sexual union (whether it is in your dreams or within waking life), an alchemy occurs. The energies of male and female merge with the dynamic oneness underlying all of reality. When you are intoxicated, in your dreams, with love and filled with passion, you have the potential for experiencing profound enlightenment. It is through the power of sexual union, all humans and all creatures come into existence. Sexual energy brings all beings into life. Sexuality is the life force, the power of evolution, liberation and transcendence. Your dreams can connect you with this powerful energy.

When I was seventeen I had a near-death experience. In those moments, when I was thought to be medically dead, I entered a realm beyond life and death. I entered a realm that had a profound influence on my life. This experience beyond death's door was one of absolute Oneness. No words can fully describe the enormity of that experience. There was no past and no future, only an endless present. There was no separation. In those moments of connectedness I knew that I was not separate from anyone or anything. There was no duality. There was an exquisite oneness with all things. The grief and longing that I felt as I realized I must leave that place and return to my life here is beyond description. I knew that I had been home.

In my private practice I have found that, even the most integrated, self-actualized people, still have a divine longing within...almost an ache. I believe this yearning is for a place that dwells deep within our psyche. It is a yearning for the forgotten Oneness with all things. In rare moments, at the point of orgasm, there is an instant where we can experience that oneness; that point beyond duality. Perhaps that is why we rush recklessly full-speed into the sexual experience. It represents that primal memory of oneness and unity. It is in that moment of orgasm we can feel a merging with spirit.

Self-survival is thought to be one of our most basic instincts. So why is it, when we see a stranger in trouble, we will jump in to help, without regard for our own physical safety? Could it be in that instant we react to an even more basic understanding? We respond to the memory, that dwells in the recesses of our mind, that we are all one. Taking a dream lover allows you to go beyond limitations and the conditioning of dualities. You can touch that primordial remembering of unity. Enlightenment and transcendence can be thought to be the goal of evolution and the ultimate destiny of each of us. Your dream lover episodes can catapult you into powerful enlightening experiences.

Here is a letter I received that provided some enlightening moments for its dreamer, Franko (real name), a young man from Australia.

Dear Denise,

As this dream began, I became aware of the smell of frangipani. To my senses it smelled wet and totally overcoming. Floating in the fragrance, my vision became alive. I found myself wandering through a lush landscape, thick with exotic vegetation. Trees and shrubs with thousands of intricate floral arrangements adorned every square inch of this landscape. Everything seemed so alive, even the grass at my feet seemed to breathe and, at the same time, caress my feet. In the distance I could hear the exhilarating sound of water flowing. Walking towards the source, I came across a towering frangipani tree with flowers as big as my face. As I got to the tree, the fragrance seemed to pick me up and caress me. In a gesture of surrender I put my face inside one of the flowers and inhaled, filling my being with incredible peace.

I heard a splash. It broke the spell. Looking towards the pool of water, I saw the tail end of what seemed to be a platypus. Excitement filled me, for I have always wanted to see a platypus face to face. Climbing over the massive root structure of the frangipani tree, a sound of humming filled my ears. To my amazement a beautiful woman appeared at the far end of the pool.

The woman was very strange. In fact her skin was blue. How could this be possible? I thought instantly of the Hindu myths and stories about blue deities. I thought, "What a blast!" Her humming continued and then stopped suddenly. She was looking straight at me or through me....or even into me. I felt myself being enveloped in a feeling of exhilarating warmth and peace. I just stood there encased in a warm cocoon of life and excitement. She began to walk towards me and the sun seemed to dance off her. It shimmered off her hair which was a tawny brown color. Her hair was alive and it bounced and tossed around her body as she moved.

I couldn't speak. I tried, but nothing audible seemed to come out. She smiled and turned and looked at the pool. All of a sudden I knew what she was here for. A knowing just took over. She touched me on the shoulder and pointed toward the way she had come. I followed her hand and through the trees I could see a crystal spire towering above the tree line in the distance. Instantly I knew it was called the City of Fountains. As I stared at the spire, I noticed every shade of color, even colors I had never seen before, spilling out of the top of the spire in a sea of light. Looking back at her, she smiled and took my hand. Slowly she began to walk towards the pool. I felt like a little puppy being led along by a loving owner.

As we touched the water a transformation began to occur. Looking at my feet, which were in the water, it was as if they were dissolving into bright energy. Without asking, I knew that my companion's name was Vanuth. As the water moved up over our bodies, we transformed to pure energy. We were completely submerged. The interior of the pool seemed to be a separate dimension. It was a dimension of light and love. Vanuth and I embraced and our bodies became one entity. Male and female were One. We made love in this state. It was a state I can hardly explain. In waking life I do know what frenzied passion and erotic seduction are all about and I can only say that it was a combination of both...and beyond. After the feelings of bliss and exhilaration, sadness crept in. The fluorescent wonderful world and my intimate partner slipped away slowly and painfully. I tried desperately to find Vanuth and her magical world but couldn't.

I then dreamed that I awoke in a type of log cabin. It was furnished in old rotten furniture and spider webs were everywhere. Looking out of a smashed window, I could see a barren deserted landscape. The remainder of a once majestic tree stood in shock before the cabin as a stark reminder of some terrible past. I kicked open the door to only reveal a decaying verandah. Out on the horizon a horrible dark cloud was rolling towards me. Lightening cracked the ground as it seemed to unleash its anger at the Earth. The cloud continued to roll forward and then spread in both directions eventually surrounding the cabin in a filthy dark electrical nightmare.

Once the circle was complete the sky seemed to crack and spew fire and lightening in every direction . Gargoyles and demons were in the center of this gross mass and then I heard a deafening scream. I stared up and froze. A creature that looked like a devil was looking down at me through the hole in the sky. He laughed and more horrible things flew my way. I closed my eyes and told myself that fear is the mind killer and nothing can exist, especially evil, if you do not believe in it.

My new wisdom was my weapon. I opened my eyes and the evil was gone. The sky was brilliant blue and the once horribly scorched earth came to life before my eyes. The ground turned green, then flowers of every color erupted into a soft breathing blanket soothing the earth. The trees grew trunks, branches and leaves and burst forth into flowers. Frangipani fragrance flooded through me once again and I knew I was on my way home. I followed a path into the distance where a faint roar could be heard. The funny thing was that the roar sounded more like a peace greeting. Millions of birds flew from the direction of the roar and buzzed and fluttered around me. In the distance I could see animals coming my way. I started to jog towards them. Elephants, giraffes, horses, deer and every kind of animal were heading down the magical path towards me. In front of the animals was a small calf; it ran up to me. Actually it wasn't running, it was dancing. Once it reached me it looked up and smiled. I was home!!! I woke up. It was about 2 am and I smiled and laughed.

Franko

In this next dream Ann Greenaway (real name) felt that she had a very spiritual experience with a dream lover.

Dear Denise,

This is a dream I had about 9 years ago. It was very vivid which is why I still remember it. You are welcome to use it in your book if you like.

The dream opens in an area of expansive green lawns with garden beds filled with flowers of many hues and perfumes. There are heavily laden fruit trees and sweet music lilts in the summer air. Many people stroll or stand talking softly. All are filled with joy. Their whole lives are joy, for this is the time when Lord Krishna lived amongst us. He illuminates our every moment with his divine presence. He is walking in the garden and I am with him. I am Radharanii, his consort. I am blissfully happy and feel so honored. Every breath brings with it a revelation.

Then the scene changes and we are alone in our private chambers. We are making love. As we embrace and unite our bodies he changes form and becomes my present day guru, Shrii Shrii Ananamurtijii. His skin and flesh are so fine and soft. It offers no resistance to my touch. Then I am enveloped in the sweetest orgasm I have ever had. Waves of exquisite pleasure permeate my entire being. So exquisite was it that I awoke. It was as though this present day Ann, whose body I now inhabit, is not allowed such sweetness.

A few months ago I was given a new Sanskrit name and guess what it is? Yes, It is Radharanii, which means "Queen who holds attraction for the Lord."

With love from Ann Greenaway

The spiritual experiences that occur in your night hours will enhance and expand your spiritual awareness in your waking hours!!! You can program your dreams for these spiritual experiences. (See the section on programming your dreams.)

SHOULD YOU FEEL GUILTY ABOUT
YOUR DREAM LOVERS?

Cassandra lies alone on the soft grass in a mountain meadow. She watches the lazy circling of a hawk overhead. Above the spiraling hawk, float large pink roses, silhouetted against the deep azure sky. Soft fragrant rose petals lightly fall from the drifting roses filling the meadow with a heady fragrance. The warm sun and the perfumed gentle breeze have put her into a mindless trance. A shadow falls across her face. Startled, she opens her eyes. Towering above her is a silent stranger. His piercing eyes and sharp features are reminiscent of a hawk, predatory and watching. Without hesitation she reaches up and slides her hands up his legs. Slowly standing, she continues to caress her hands across his finely muscled chest and up and over his shoulders. She buries her nose in the flesh of his neck and inhales him like fine powder. He turns his head, surrendering his stoic masked mien, and smiles. Eagles screech from all the hidden ledges. Rampant thunder. Sliding down to the verdant tapestry like a captive creature, possessed at last, she rises again and again in ecstasy...and is brought to a shuddering stillness.

Cassandra awakes with a jolt. Her husband Phil is snoring softly beside her. It is raining outside. She feels terrified and guilty about her dream. Phil may not be perfect but she does love him. So why would she dream of someone else? Phil shifts his body in sleep and reaches out towards her. Cassandra closes her eyes tightly and turns away.

Many people feel guilty about sexual dreams.

35

Unable to control the range and content of these nocturnal activities, they block out the memory of many dreams and feel shocked by some of the dreams that <u>are</u> remembered. They anxiously wonder what these images of forbidden sexual pleasures mean.

This fearful, repressive response to sexual dreams comes directly out of a long tradition of body/mind separation in Judeo-Christian culture. According to this tradition, the mind is good but the body is evil. In the most extreme interpretation, all sex is sinful unless it is directly tied to procreation purposes. There is no place for pleasure.

Although most people now consciously reject this position, remnants of these beliefs persist in the emotional response to sexual dreams. We may act in a new way, tell ourselves it's O.K., and yet continue to feel guilty. By contrast, ancient metaphysical cultures and Eastern religions considered sex to be an integral part of human nature and experience. Sex was not in conflict with religion or spirituality. Sexual performance was practiced as an art and included as a normal part of each person's education. Pre-Christian classical statues and Indian and Oriental art frequently depict scenes of explicit, sexual pleasure where lovers gaze at one another in sweet ecstasy; free from shame, fear or guilt.

At first glance, it may seem that pursuing sexual experience-even in the dream state-could easily bring feelings of guilt. Exploring these thoughts and feelings can actually bring awareness of unresolved beliefs and behavior patterns that have crippled or deadened your experience of life. The experience of guilt can inhibit normal adult functioning and can severely limit your sexual enjoyment. Guilt is <u>always</u> disruptive.

In my twenty years experience as a healer I have found that one of the biggest blocks to healing is an attachment to guilt. In fact, many major physical imbalances, from cancer to arthritis, often have their emotional source in guilt. Sexual guilt can be processed and released in your dreams. By working through feelings of guilt about sexual dreams, a person can be freed for much fuller enjoyment of life.

It is helpful to remember in guilt-releasing work that guilt can serve a specific purpose in a person's life. By feeling guilty, a person may continue to act in ways labeled "bad" but, by feeling guilty, still consider himself or herself to be a "good" person. Feeling guilty about dream sex or past sexual relationships can also be a way of avoiding relationships or not confronting a fear of intimacy or a fear of rejection.

Paradoxically, feeling guilty involves <u>not</u> taking responsibility. A responsible person says,"Yes, I did that and it was painful." Guilt does not accept either the fact or the act of the pain. It denies both. The guilty person says, "Well, I didn't mean to and it wasn't my fault...."

Guilt is <u>choosing</u> not to forgive yourself. It is essential that you forgive yourself for your past. To do this you must be willing to accept yourself for what you have done in the past. When you judge yourself for things that you have done in the past you are looking backwards, you are not looking inward. To look inward is to know that everything you have ever experienced was necessary for your growth and self-understanding. It was necessary for you to be who you are today. Even the thoughts and actions you regret or feel ashamed of, contribute to your being who you are today. As uncomfortable as those memories are, it is important to observe and release them. Forgive yourself. If you feel judgement about your past, it controls you in the present. When you recognize that everything you have ever experienced was necessary for your growth and each event in your life, whether pleasant or painful, has shaped you bit by bit into the person you are now, then the guilt will begin to disappear. As you accept and totally embrace each of your dream lovers, you will be releasing past sexual guilt and your waking sexuality will be more free and joyous.

It is perfectly normal to have sexual feelings towards almost anyone within your dreams. Remember, no matter who or what you are feeling an attraction to (it can be a friend or a stranger, or even an animal or innate object), it is symbolic of an aspect of yourself and thus it is perfectly normal to feel that attraction. Your dream lovers are merely various aspects of self that need to be integrated and loved. Release censorship of yourself. There is no such thing as promiscuity or incest in your dreams. These dream images are simply different aspects of yourself appearing in erotic form. Your father, in a dream, may simply be an archetypal image for authority and strength. Your brother may represent family affection. It is not uncommon for women to have dreams of fathers and brothers mixed up with dreams of husbands and lovers. It can simply be that these dreams show that the women are transferring their love from their childhood family to a new family of their own.

The woman who gave me this dream was very disturbed by it.

My older brother and I have always been very close-very good friends. The one time he had ever shown any (slight) sexual attraction to me was when he was about 13 and I was 11. Now, years later I always feel that he is trying to find another me in his wives. He is on his second wife. It sounds very egotistical but I believe it is true.

Any way, my brother came for a stay at my family home and then it happened. It must have been dawn when a startling dream awoke me. It was only short but very potent. I dreamt that there was an enormous penis floating in the air above my bed. I was being asked to come to him. (I knew it was my brother.) He was promising me a beautiful sexual relationship. I agreed to go with him. Then a big round, wise face came between us which told me not to go. I then thought, "No I won't go."

When I awoke I was rather distressed at myself for agreeing to go in the first place. I feel that maybe I agreed because he is having a non-loving, relationship with his 2nd wife. The dream was very real and my brother must have (subconsciously) remembered it as he gave me a very loving cuddle that morning when he came out. We have a friendly brotherly/sisterly relationship. It is definitely not a lover-type of relationship.

This dream does not necessarily mean that there is a subconscious desire for an incestuous relationship. Having an incestuous dream almost never indicates that those feelings have any reality in waking life. This dream could mean that she is balancing her male and female aspects within. Her brother may have been the closest male to her. It would be natural that he would symbolize her own male aspect and it would be natural that she would subconsciously choose him to represent her male side. It could also mean that she had some concern for her brother and she wanted to give him love. Sex is a powerful symbol that can represent giving love. This dream could even come from a past life connection where they had been together as lovers. In any event there is no cause for concern, shame or guilt.

It is necessary to forgive oneself in order to achieve full sexual union in the present. The more you can acknowledge the full range of sexual elements present in your dreams, the more integrated and whole your self will be. Move towards pleasure in your dreams. Embrace dream pleasure and you will find your waking life more balanced.

Here is a dream that a woman sent to me that shows the joy of dreaming without guilt.

Denise,

I finally had an erotic dream! It was very nice and worthwhile. I was paid $10,000 each time for my services!!! And my services were much sought after. It was a very pleasant way to earn heaps. I wasn't aware *that you could make that much money and have such a good time from such very nice fellas. I felt no regrets or embarrassment at all. I was just extremely pleased with myself."*

You can recognize, work through and release guilt through your dreams. Here is an exercise you can use in regard to your sexual dreams. If you have a sexual dream about which you feel uncomfortable or guilty, write it down in detail. After you have done this, say to yourself gently, but with conviction, "I accept who I am and what I have done and what others have done to me. I accept and forgive myself and others."

Go over the dream you wrote and identify what you gain by continuing to feel guilty about each part. Then go back over your dream and visualize it slowly, integrating and recognizing each part of the dream symbolizes an aspect of yourself. Repeat the visualization as many times as necessary to be comfortable with it, each time releasing more of the guilt. Finally, you can burn what you have written about these guilt-ridden dreams saying, "I release now and forevermore my attachments to this guilt. So be it."

For example: perhaps you dream that you are making love with a very aggressive soldier. You feel guilty about the dream because you don't like aggression and war. Going over the dream you might recognize that the soldier symbolizes authority to you. In your job you have felt like the office punching bag. The dream symbolizes that you need to take more authority in your life and stand up for yourself. The dream is allowing you to align with your own authority. Making love with an aggressive soldier in your dreams will help you to do just that. Go over the dream until you feel no guilt-then burn it.

If you still are plagued by guilt then go back into the dream and change it. Imagine the dream again but alter the circumstances, so that you can become more comfortable with it. For example change the soldier to a Peace Corp Volunteer. Reframe the dream in your mind.

HOW TO ENTER A LOVER'S DREAMS

Sam finds himself walking down a spiraling golden staircase; round and round until he steps unto a great grassy plain. A warm wind ruffles the tall grasses like a whimsical zephyr across a great green sea. A short distance away stands his girl friend, Rachel. The folds of her white translucent chiffon dress ripple in the breeze. Thinly veiled, her creamy moon breasts rise and fall majestically with her every breath. Sam is awed by the magnificent power radiating from those alabaster glowing orbs. Mesmerized, and feeling like a God, with his virile shaft of resplendent energy, he approaches this luminescent Goddess. He reaches out and gently cradles her breasts. Full and round, they are heavy like overripe fruit ready to drop. The hot underside of each pliant breast sends pulsing fire up his arms and through his body as he buries his face in the depths of her cleavage.

The next morning, as they lay in bed, Rachel told Sam that she had a strange dream. She dreamed that she was on a wide plain dressed in a white flowing dress. She said Sam was there too, and he seemed to have a great fascination for her breasts.

This type of dreaming (where you and another actually share the same dream) is called dream sharing. It is not unusual. In the case of Sam and Rachel it happened spontaneously, but it is an ability that can be cultivated. You can literally share a dream with a loved one. This exercise is enhanced if you are sleeping together because your auras are so intermingled. It is then easier to step into each other's dreams. Dream sharing can also be done from a distance. If you are separated from your loved one, it can be a way to continue your intimacy. For the most effective dream sharing to occur, it is valuable to discuss it beforehand. Mutually agree to enter each other's dreams. As you go to sleep, affirm, with intention, that you and your partner will be together in your dreams. Often dream sharing occurs spontaneously without pre-programming. Perhaps you have had an experience of sharing a dream with your lover. The following morning you discover that you both experienced a similar dream. Dream sharing can be an excellent way to increase intimacy and to develop greater understanding within relationships.

Before beginning your dream sharing, it is valuable to do a simple meditation. This meditation is based on a Tantric Buddhist technique. First, sit in a comfortable position directly facing your partner. Make sure your spine is straight. This is extremely important for this particular meditation. Now, participate in a very natural type of breathing. As you inhale your abdomen expands and as you exhale, your abdomen contracts. If you sense your chest expanding and contracting instead of your abdomen, simply imagine the presence of a balloon in the center of your abdomen. The balloon expands and contracts with each breath. It may take a short while to become accustomed to this type of breathing, however the results will be well worth it! It is a very natural way of breathing; this is the way you breath when you are asleep.

After you allow yourself to feel very relaxed, imagine a current of energy originating in the center of the earth moving up through your spine and all the way up through your entire being. This is your grounding cord. Imagine this energy moving out the top of your head like a geyser, cascading down around you like a fountain. Look into the left eye of your partner and imagine a beam of energy flowing out from your own heart chakra (the energy center in the middle of the chest) into the heart chakra of your partner. Then imagine this same energy moving down his/her spine and penetrating the sex chakra. This extremely potent energy then travels from your partner's sexual area into your own, arriving in your heart chakra once again. This is called the "circle of gold" technique. You may also reverse the flow of the energy. As you are doing this, allow yourself to experience the very deep and profound connection with your partner. Once you have completed this exercise, maintain silence and immediately go to sleep, programming yourself for an even deeper connection to occur during the night.

Another technique from Tantric Buddhist tradition, is the use of erotic visualization. To engage in this practice, sit in a meditative pose across from each other and visualize yourself to be an aspect of God. From Hindu texts, "The Goddess resides in all women, the Lord resides in all men." The woman, breathing in a very deep relaxed manner, visualizes herself to be the erotic Goddess. She sees herself beautiful, filled with vigor and life. Perhaps dancing and moving in harmony with the pulse of life. Music is excellent to use in conjunction with this exercise. Some use the image of the Gopis dancing with Krishna, but use your imagination and be creative. This Goddess of love, that is imagined, is a symbol of intuition, inner sight and wisdom, and the giver of life. The man visualizes himself to embody power and prowess...a God of love. He visualizes himself radiating incredible strength.

All mystical traditions make use of visualization for psychic transformation. For a couple, a most important visualization is to see each other as God and Goddess, or in other words, to see each other as exalted. An early Hindu text says that those who worship respectively on the altar of love will be granted their desires. It says, "Think of the sexual region of a woman as a sacrificial altar, her hairs as sacrificial grass, her skin as the elixir dispenser, the two lips of her yoni (labia) as the tongues of flame that rise up from the offering." Visualization is a powerful tool to experience the alchemy of love and to prepare for dream sharing.

Here is a guided visualization aimed at contributing to sharing dreams with your partner. It will also allow you to feel more responsive and receptive to your own sexuality so that you feel more fulfillment, more love, and a deeper connection to spirit. To prepare the room for this meditation, make sure that the room you use is clean, beautiful, comfortable, and warm. The room should feel conscious, as if the things in the room are cared for and loved. Unplug the phone. You might even put flowers, incense and candles around to contribute to the very special intimate atmosphere that you are creating.

Record this meditation on tape, to play before bed. This will help your dream sharing efforts.

You might consider using soothing sensuous music in the background and speaking in a soothing voice.

For this meditation, you must sit in a comfortable position. Sit across from your partner. Make sure that your spine is straight. Take a deep breath in and hold this breath. Keep holding. Keep holding. And very slowly release.
Good. And again. Take an even deeper breath. Hold this breath and as you hold...feel your body relaxing...just letting go. Good. Now release that breath and relax even more.

Good. Now take an another deep, deep breath and hold. While you are holding, feel your body relaxing and letting go. even more hold... hold... and now, through your mouth, slowly release. Let it all out. Good. Now, one more deeeeep, deeeeep breath,...hold...hold...hold...and release. Good. And one last deep, deep breath. With each breath you are becoming more and more relaxed, your mind is opening to the positive and powerful suggestions that it is given. Release... let go. All your concerns are releasing as you exhale. You are beginning to feel more and more relaxed. As you travel through your body, relaxing each part, the chi, or electromagnetic energy that circulates through you, flows stronger and clearer.

Now, move your awareness into your left foot. Imagine that your left foot is completely filled with bright light...shimmering, golden light. As this light bathes your left foot, your foot is relaxing even more. Your left foot is now completely relaxed. Good. Now watch (or if you are not visual, perceive or be aware of) as that golden light fills your right foot, completely filling the entire right foot. Now feel as your right foot relaxes...let it go. Good. Now, let it go even more. Good. Now move with your awareness into both of your feet. Your feet are now completely filled with golden, shimmering, brilliant light. This light is vibrating and circulating quickly. Feel as your feet relax...and relax even more. Your feet are now completely relaxed. Completely relaxed. So loose, so limp, so lazy. Be aware of feeling that light surging up to fill your legs, from the tips of your toes to your hip sockets, all filled with golden light. Now be aware of your your legs feeling very relaxed and yet vibrating with energy.

Good. Now, like a slow wave, the light fills your lower abdomen, middle abdomen, upper chest. Take three deep breaths...each breath vitalizes and fills your torso...your entire torso...there is only golden light circulating, bathing, relaxing and vitalizing your entire torso. You may do this now. Good. Now let that light spill down into your left arm...all the way to the tips of your fingers. Feel as your arm pulsates with life force swirling energies...healing energies. Good. Now let that golden light spill down your right arm. The tips of your fingers may begin to feel warm and tingly. That's good. It means that you can feel that dynamic energy as it is surging through you. Your arms are now completely relaxed and resting easily. Very good.

Now take a breath, and as you breathe pull the golden light into your head. This golden light fills your head and spills out the top of your head. It spills out through that point called the thou-

sand petal lotus, in the very center of your head. Now your entire body is relaxed and feeling good. You are ready to begin your inner journey that will open those incredible healing, vitalizing energies within you. It is a journey that will allow you to be more responsive and receptive to entering the dreams of your partner.

Look into the left eye of your partner. (That is the eye that is on the same side as your right hand.) As you continue to look into the left eye, put your awareness in that area of your body called the perineum (that point between your anus and your genitals). You are looking at your partner but your awareness is focused on your perineum. (Have dual concentration.) Radiate your awareness out in all directions from your perineum about three inches. Breath into this area. Visualize this area to be a clear crimson color...so vivid...much the color of a deep red rose. And with each breath this area is becoming intensely warm and vibrantly energized. As you listen to the voice on this tape keep breathing into your groin area. The powerful inner-fire, the kundalini, the serpent power, is awakening as you breathe into your genitals. This energy is so called the serpent power because of the way it cycles up the spine, similar to the circular movement of a serpent. The ancient Greeks knew that a powerful potent healing power lay in this area, thus the intertwined snakes for the Hippocratic Medical Symbol of Health. Breathe into this area... each breath is vitalizing your body. Enjoy the feelings that you have in this area while you continue to look into the eye of your partner . You have a short while to do this.

Good. Now imagine that coming up from the earth and through your first chakra (your genital area) is your grounding cord. This cord connects you to the earth and allows you to feel balanced and stable. This cord of energy circles up through your first chakra and enters your second chakra. Visualize this area to be a brilliant orange, much like the orange of the California poppy. This is your area of feeling and it lies just a few inches below your navel, called the hara or tanden in the Orient. In the ancient Orient, this area was considered to be the center of the universe. Zen Buddhists would breathe into this area as a way to attain enlightenment. As this area is opened and cleared, your emotions are balanced and unblocked and you are able to feel and express that feeling freely. You have a while to center on this area. Breathing into it easily. Each breath empowers this area. Continue to have eye contact with your partner.

Good. Now move into the third chakra. This is the area around your diaphragm/spleen . The energy from your grounding cord is circulating up and filling this area. Imagine this area as the brilliance of yellow...a sunflower slightly waving in the breeze on a warm, lazy summer day. This area represents thoughtfulness and intelligence. As this area is cleared, your thought processes have clarity and wisdom. Let your breath fill this area. Intensify the color and the feeling with each breath. You may do this now.

Good. Now, in a surge, feel as the grounding cord moves into the heart chakra, which is the energy center in the middle of the chest. What power fills you as this area opens! See, feel, perceive the verdant color of green of a forest within your heart area. Green represents life, it is the bridge between the lower chakras and the upper chakras. This area represents love. It's no accident that when someone is in love they say, "My heart is singing." or "My heart is so full." We intuitively know that this area is connected with love. As you experience this area, really let that pulsating feeling of love envelope you. Feel the flame of love radiate from this area of your body. You have a moment to do this. Really feel it.

Good. Now let that increasing vibrancy fill your throat area. The color associated with this energy is blue. Imagine the blue of the iris so clear, so vivid. This area rules communication. All that you communicate comes from truth and clarity. You speak your mind lovingly and clearly. All your intimate relationships are enhanced by your communications. Take a short while to add potency to this area.

Good. Now allow that energy to move up into the third eye, the area between and slightly above your eyes. Imagine a tiny ball of purple light about the size of a pea in this area. The third eye relates to your intuition. It is your connection to your inner spirit and your inner life. Let the light radiate from your third eye, and breathe deeply into this area, each breath increases your intuition and ability to perceive inner dimensions. You may do this now.

Very good. Now, expand your awareness to include the top of your head, the thousand petaled lotus. Imagine this area is radiating the color white, the same purity of a lotus. This is your connection to spirit. Feel joy and inner peace filling and circulating through this area.

Excellent. Now all your chakras, and each of your partner's chakras have been activated. Imagine energy radiating from each of your chakras to each corresponding chakra of your partner while you maintain eye contact. Take a while to do this.

Now, to increase your connection to your partner you are about to begin what is called the Breath of Fire. It is called the Breath of Fire because it is a purifying breath. This breath increases virility in a man and is rejuvenating for a woman. This is an especially potent exercise. As you do this exercise across from your partner, the circulation of life force energy between you becomes very intense. Start with a slow even breath synchronizing with your partner's breath.. The breath then becomes faster and faster. Be sure to continue to synchronize your breathing as the rhythm becomes faster and faster. This breath will begin to merge your energy and the energy of your partner thus preparing you for dream sharing.

(You can leave a space in the tape to do the Breath of Fire.)

Now, begin taking slower easier synchronized breaths. This is important.

(Leave some space on the tape for these slow easy breathes.)

Your energy is now very connected with your

partner. Without speaking, prepare for bed, saying to yourself, "Tonight I share dreams with my lover and I remember my dreams!" Sweet Dreams!!!

USING DREAM LOVERS TO FIND
YOUR SOULMATES

The very word soulmate evokes images of Romeo and Juliet, Cleopatra and Mark Antony, Tristan and Isolde and Katherine Hepburn and Spencer Tracy. It evokes images of a most exquisite love that seems to transcend time and space-a precious, unending love that wafts throughout time with two people finding their absolute perfect complement in each other.

What is a soulmate? How can you recognize a soulmate? Can your dream lover be a key to discovering your soulmate? What is the difference between a soulmate and a love-mate? How can your dreams help you find your perfect match? The mushrooming of dating services and 'personals' indicates the overpowering urgency towards finding that perfect mate. Even those already within a satisfactory relationship often talk about a yearning or restlessness for something more.

Although the term 'soulmates' in common terminology can be used to describe the one passionate love of your life, soulmates can also be described as all of those individuals that you have been with, time after time, in past lives. This idea is based on the reincarnation theory that you incarnate lifetime after lifetime with other like-minded individuals. These souls can be likened to a great flock of birds that travel to distant countries, yet always fly together. I have found consistently, based on information gathered in my reincarnation seminars, that individuals often incarnate as a group and tend to be drawn together lifetime after lifetime. Often these individuals will stay in touch through the dream states even if they don't know each other in this life.

A striking example of a group of souls incarnating together occurred in Canberra, the capital of Australia. A show of hands after a reincarnation process indicated that over two-thirds of the hundred people in the room felt that, during the regression, they had experienced a past life in Rome. Upon examination, it seemed plausible that those individuals who had a past life in ancient Rome, (a planned city that was a center for government that was peopled by many government employees), would have chosen to incarnate in Canberra, (a planned city that is a center for government that is peopled by many government employees).

A personal example of the Group Soul Theory occurred for me as a young university student in the Midwest of the United States. I had been very much in love with a university professor and we shared a small country home. Sensing that he was seeing another woman, I became distraught and packed my bags and moved to Hawaii to put the soured love affair behind me. A second move in Hawaii placed me in the tropical university district of Manoa Valley. A friendly neighbor brought by some freshly baked bread to welcome me to the area. Over tea, as we shared our backgrounds, we both discovered that we had gone to the same large university in the Midwest. It even turned out that we knew some of the same people. As she began talking about a clandestine affair she had had with a college professor, the truth slowly dawned upon me. It became clear that I was speaking to none other than my previously unknown Nemesis. She was the woman with whom my lover had had an affair. Luckily the situation was far enough behind us that we eventually became the best of friends.

There is a tendency to think that our soulmates are only those individuals whom we meet and have an instant affinity for in this life. However, I have found in my regression work that soulmates can also be those people whom we have difficulties with in our present lives. In fact, those very challenging individuals often are those with whom we have had the most intimate past-life connections.

Understanding the concept of karma can make these seemingly negative soulmates more understandable. Karma is the idea that what you sow, you reap. Your harvest is not necessarily dictated by a governing deity but rather by your own sense of integrity. Have you ever told a lie and then immediately stubbed your toe or walked into the wall? We have an internal set of checks and balances and we are always wanting to make sure that the scales are balanced. Hence we reap according to our own inner sense of right and wrong. If we feel that we have cheated someone financially, often we will, subconsciously, make sure that we are deprived of an equal amount of money in one way or another. This idea of karma applies to past lives as well, so that, for example, if you use your physical strength to bully others in one life, the next life you might choose to incarnate into a weak body as a way to gain compassion for others.

When there is some lesson that you want to learn you are like a broad spectrum broadcasting station on Soul Level Network. For example you might broadcast, 'I need to learn humility. Is there anyone out there who will teach me humility?' Someone who is not deeply connected to you on a soul level will just walk on by... not wanting to waste part of the incarnational experience teaching you a lesson. However, it is that individual who has loved you deeply on a soul level, a soulmate, that will resignedly shrug and say, "OK, I'll take the job this time. I love you enough to give you the experience that you feel you need". I have found repeatedly, in my personal regression work, that the individuals my clients claim to have the most difficulty with are the very individuals whom they discover they have loved the most deeply in the past.

How do you recognize a soulmate? Often there is a rapport or recognition. If there has been a sexual liaison in a past life, there will be a tendency for a physical attraction to occur in the present life, sometimes almost explosively intense. Though soulmates don't always see things eye to eye there is, nevertheless, usually a sense of familiarity that accompanies the relationship, a communication beyond explanation, a deep attachment negatively or positively and sometimes even telepathy. Soulmates can be parents, children, business associates friends and lovers.

Perhaps one of the deepest esoteric teachings is the idea that each human being has a perfect mate waiting to be discovered. This person has been called a lovemate, dualmate, twinmate or soulmate. Researchers have stated that even within the 'The Old Religion' (or the Stone Age religion) one of the main reasons for leading a useful life was so that one could be reborn near his or her loved one again in the next life. Johann Wolfgang von Goethe wrote a novel based on the medieval idea that couples were divinely united. The book, called *Die Wahlverwandtschaften* , which means 'elective affinities' contends that every individual has a perfect mate waiting to be discovered.

Edgar Cayce, a trance medium who gave extensive information regarding soulmates, cautioned, however, against leaving one's marriage partner because of an attraction to someone who seemed to be a lovemate. He felt that people had much to learn in the context of marriage even if sometimes there was friction. He further pointed out that even if you find your lovemate, it might not necessarily guarantee a good marriage. Cayce felt that in order to find your lovemate, it was necessary to find peace within oneself first. He stated, "Those abiding by the laws of the Lord will meet and marry their true soulmates. Those who defied God's law will be denied this union. Impunity kept soulmates apart, morality brought them together." It must be remembered that Cayce was a very strong Christian and came from a strong Bible-abiding background.

Elizabeth Clare Prophet, a spiritual teacher, recalled her meeting with the man whom she felt was her lovemate. She was a young woman attending Boston University in eastern United States and felt compelled to attend a lecture being given by Mark Prophet, a man 20 years her senior. The next day the man said, "You and I are twin flames and we will work together until my death."

Being uncertain, she asked for a sign, which was forthcoming. As she was dressing, she looked in the mirror and she seemed to see Mark's face. She said, "It was ancient. I saw that I was the reflection in the negative (feminine) polarity of that positive (masculine) image." They eventually married and worked together until Mark's death.

A commonly held theory regarding lovemates is that we were originally androgynous beings, souls that were neither male nor female. Somewhere in time, this soul was split into two halves; a male and female. These two halves set forth unto the earth plane (a dimension of polarities) to grow and expand, forever striving to reunite again. The constant drive towards procreation is seen as a deep spiritual urge for that primal union, for the experience of oneness that occurred before the separation.

Those who hold this theory contend that there will be a greater increase in the searching for and reuniting with our soulmates and lovemates in the coming years because of the increase in the vibratory rate of the planet. This theory, reuniting of soulmates and lovemates, also accounts for the increase in the non-traditional relationships that transcend differences in race, age, sex, religion and social standing. Sometimes lovemates will be much older or younger than their match or they will have different races or socioeconomic standing. Yet the urge to be together is stronger than society's values.

Sometimes, one or the other of the lovemates can be in the spirit world, rather than in a physical body, giving assistance from the other side. This accounts for a child's 'invisible' playmates or an adult's feeling that there is someone watching over him or her. Lovemates can even be of the same sex, though one will usually have the negative (feminine) polarity within and the other will have the positive (masculine) polarity.

We often have the idea that when we meet our "love mate" he or she will be perfect and we won't ever have to speak because we know each other's heart so well. We see each other across a crowded room and the bells peal and the birds sing. Ha!!

Usually when lovemates meet (unless they have worked on themselves), they will find that it is difficult to get along . Because a lovemate is the other half of you anything that you don't like in yourself will be stimulated by them! In fact the relationship can be quite stormy because your lovemate will be your mirror. He or she will emphasize or reflect back to you those areas of yourself with which you aren't satisfied. These relationships can be very exciting but can also be tumultuous. For that reason, when lovemates come together, the relationship isn't always enduring. If they can survive the test of time (usually several years or more) they are amazing relationships. However, when lovemates unite, for whatever duration, there is a true mating of the heart and the soul that is fathomless.

The film, *Made in Heaven*, with Timothy Hutton and Kelly McGinnis shows Timothy as a soul who decides to incarnate into the earth plane to reunite with his true love who has also just incarnated. His guardian angel warns him that he will forget this goal once he hits the earth plane. Timothy assures the angel that he will remember. As both Timothy and Kelly grow older in different parts of the country, each has a dull, undefined ache or urging for some undefined goal. They both have consciously forgotten their quest to find each other. Often, throughout their lives, there are times when they are in the same place at the same time but they just miss each other. (Often, in my private practice, I have found that lovemates will be in the same places at the same time, though not known to each other.) At the movie's conclusion they each gain a sense of self-respect and self-love and they finally reunite.

The degree to which you accept and love yourself is the degree to which you will find your lovemate. When you are trying to attract your lovemate, if you feel unworthy of love, your mind will say, "There must be something wrong with this person if he or she loves me." Then you will subconsciously begin to find things wrong with the other person and push him or her away. Your lovemate can even be the person you have been married to for 20 years but you didn't have the inner eyes to see.

Tips for Finding Your Lovemate

1. Program your dreams to encounter and connect with your soulmate!!! Lovemates often appear in dreams before they physically appear in your life. It's not unusual for lovemates to have the same dream on the same night, even before they meet. In your dreams he or she might not always look the same as in waking life but there will be something about him or her that will "feel" the same. You can program your dreams by saying before bed, "Tonight I meet my lovemate in my dreams."

2. Enjoy yourself in waking life. Laugh, communicate freely, develop many friendships.

3. Relax. Take the time to take pleasure in the small things in life.

4. Begin to find a balance with the male and female aspects of yourself. Find a balance between giving and receiving, activity and rest, thinking and feeling. As your male and female aspects align within yourself, your physical male or female complement can align with you.

5. Involve yourself in activities of the heart.

6. When separation from others in life occurs, begin to see this as a valuable, dynamic, wholesome experience. Begin to see relationships as a dance. First you dance with one partner and then swirl to another with no disappointment of leaving one to enjoy the next. Your fear of separation can keep your lovemate away.

7. Begin to see, in each individual whom you meet, an aspect of yourself. See yourself in

everyone.

8. Visualize your perfect partner. Write down, in detail, all the qualities you want in your ideal mate. Put this list on the wall in a location where you can begin to program your subconscious mind for this relationship. <u>And</u> be willing to accept your lovemate in whatever form he or she appears.

9. Ask God/Great Spirit/your Higher Self for guidance to find your lovemate.

10. Tie up loose ends in your life. (Complete anything that pulls on your energy.)

11. Enjoy your life and your relationships exactly the way they are now. There are very few princes and princesses out there but there are a lot of frogs waiting to be kissed. One of those frogs could be your lovemate. Start kissing frogs and enjoying it. Have fun! I have found it is very difficult to pull your lovemate to you if you are dissatisfied with your life. A joyous, satisfied person is very appealing.

12. Suspend your restrictions about the way your lovemate will come to you and what form the relationship will take.

13. Love yourself and do things that allow you to love life.

14. Expect a miracle!

HOW TO HAVE ASTRAL
DREAM LOVERS

Rhonda finally fell asleep after restlessly tossing and turning from one end of her bed to another. Shortly after falling asleep, she began to feel a subtle vibration as she lightly lifted out of her body. She found herself floating about five feet above the bed. She noticed the ceiling was made of long wooden panels. She thought it was funny that she had never really noticed the ceiling before. Taking a deep breath she floated closer to the ceiling, pushing herself up and down with her fingers on the paneling. Twisting and even somersaulting as she lay on her back, she cruised up and down again and again. It all felt so easy and so light. She was elated, laughing and happy. Almost bursting with excitement, she held out her hands. They seemed luminescent and glowing. Half floating, half walking away from the bed, she turned around to glimpse her sleeping form. She was only slightly curious to observe her own body resting in bed.

Floating through the bedroom door, out over the veranda and into the garden, Rhonda gently flew over the tree tops. Looking down as she sailed over house tops and roof tops, everything was bathed in a soft glowing light. It was as if the world had been blanketed in liquid moonlight. Rapidly floating towards her was a large silvery orb light mass. She somehow knew that this shimmering orb of light was a male energy form. A surge of sexual desire rippled through her as she found herself drawn closer to this pulsing energy mass. An image of a man's face flashed in her mind...a man that she had known slightly in the past but to whom she had felt very attracted. She intuitively felt that this light form was that former acquaintance. As their light forms touched, they merged. Each breath became a pulse that shaped itself to the other. Bodies shaping themselves to each other. Bending, dancing, joining, touching all the forbidden corners of the soul. The closing and opening of light. The shuddering of a brilliant dawn; the stillness of a shadowed dusk...the breath from the lungs of the universe. "I love you" echoed through the black velvet of the night.

Three weeks after this very vivid dream Rhonda ran into her former acquaintance. Unlike his normal reserved demeanor he acted as if he was meeting a long lost friend. He asked Rhonda out for coffee. They began to date, though it was a few months before Rhonda told him of her nocturnal experience. Although he didn't consciously remember the meeting, his altered attitude alleged a subconscious remembering of a chance meeting among the stars.

Astral travel can be a unique and valuable addition to your dream lover adventures. When I was a child I was always leaping from the end of my bed, tumbling and flying through mid-air. I really believed that I could fly. I didn't know that I was astral traveling. As I got older, I forgot the ability to consciously fly. In my dreams, however, there were relics of this abandoned memory. Occasionally, I would discover myself in a dream soaring over the rooftops and racing to the stars. In my twenties, I enrolled in a week-long course focusing on astral travel. There, I was once again able to reclaim a degree of that skill which had given me such great joy as a child.

There is one category of dream experience not included in most definitions of dreaming. It is commonly referred to as an "out-of-body" experience. An out-of-body experience is one where the awareness of your soul is literally separated from your physical body. This usually occurs during sleep. Numerous esoteric religions and philosophies are founded on this experience. In addition to a sense of separation from the physical body, there is also a self-awareness which is extremely vivid. This is quite different from a dream, though it is not uncommon. In fact, during sleep, the sensation of a quick jolt might be indicative of a difficult re-entry into your body. Individuals often have out-of-body experiences, yet fail to recall them.

Dreams about flying or being in an airplane frequently accompany out-of-body experiences. Also, individuals who actually fly or are pilots in waking life are often inclined toward out-of-body experiences. Research indicates that people who, as children, felt they could fly, or spent time jumping off objects such as trees, also have a tendency toward out-of-body experiences.

There are records of out-of-body experiences occurring throughout history. Descriptions of these experiences are similar whether they took place in India, Egypt, South America or even in the Mid-Western United States. Vivid out-of-body experiences are frequently triggered by an accident or a near-death experience.

These experiences can be generated by a deliberate attempt to consciously leave the body. Most people find that these experiences dramatically alter their belief concerning the nature of personal reality. They also tend to be extremely joyous experiences for the recipients. They are not that uncommon. In fact, specific studies reflect that at least 25 percent of adult humans recall having at least one out-of-body experience in their lifetime. Many did not realize that they were having out-of-body experiences until the phenomenon was defined for them.

There appears to be no research of any kind indicating that damage may result from a person consciously leaving his body. In truth, it is a very natural occurrence. An interesting occurrence in connection with the out-of-body experience is that, when you are in this frame of reference, you do not experience time or space as you generally know it to be. Another interesting phenomenon is that you may notice when you first leave your body, you seem to remain in substance very much in your present physical form. However, the longer you are separated from your physical body, the weaker that memory becomes, and your "being" appears to transcend into a cloud-like vapor or some other amorphous form.

There are certain variables which seem to influence the out-of-body experience. Alcohol appears to be a definite deterrent to experiencing this phenomenon. One thing that seems to increase the ability to leave the body is the way you position your body, particularly if you lie in the magnetic north/south direction with your head to the north. The north/south alignment is also valuable in regard to sleeping deeply. If you desire a very restful night's sleep, placing your head toward the magnetic north is ideal. However, if you want to feel energized, placing your head toward south works best. For astral travel your head should be toward the north.

Oliver Fox, in his book, *Astral Travel*, speaks of his own experience. "Instantly, the vividness of life increases a hundredfold. Never had sea and sky and trees shown with such glamorous beauty. Even the commonplace houses seemed alive and mystically beautiful. Never had I felt so absolutely well, so clear-brained, so divinely powerful, so inexpressibly free! The sensation was exquisite beyond words."

When I initially began astral traveling, I would remain close to my home. I would astrally wander through the different rooms in our house. Curiously, my traveling would often be in a different time frame, it would be daylight instead of evening. The astral dimension is an arena that is outside of the space/time continuum. As I gained more confidence I began to experience floating and eventually flying. At the start, I would venture only a few feet above the ground because I still retained the fear of my physical body falling. As I grew in my skill, I was spreading wings and transcending the earth in an ecstasy of flight.

My first adult recollection of astral travel was a frightening one. It was a very humid, tropical night in Hawaii. Early one evening, I spent time with a good friend casually discussing the art of astral travel. This was an activity in which neither of us had participated. We jokingly said we would meet each other at 3:00 a.m., selecting a pre-determined location. Before I retired, I said to myself, "Tonight, I will meet Susan at 3:00 a.m. by the waterfall in the upper Manoa Valley." This was a good midpoint area with which we were both familiar.

It was about 3:00 a.m., I awoke aware of a very strange sensation. Although the room was dark, I felt a kind of rocking, floating experience as if I were drifting on a float tube in a swimming pool. I was startled. The ceiling which is normally six to seven feet above my bed was now only inches from my body. I was weightless...without substance. What was this? What was happening? I couldn't quite understand why I was hovering so near the ceiling. Was it a dream? No, I was fully conscious. Yet, it seemed so very real. I was so light, so free. Then almost as an afterthought, I rolled over gently, noticing my bed was below...with me in it! The terror of observing my own body was so frightening that I immediately zoomed back into my body with a harsh jolt. The shock was so profound that it took a long time before I ventured out again.

It was as if I was split into two different persons. The part of me that I identify as "who I am", was free, light and floating. The other "being", the part that I associate with my physical body, was somehow me, but not me, lying on the bed, a mere physical shell. This experience was only the beginning of many explorations into the nature of astral travel and out-of-body adventures.

Shamans, American Indians and African witch doctors have all practiced rituals enabling them to escape from their physical bodies. The Australian aborigines would go into a trance and venture on an astral journey whenever their tribes needed guidance. When I gave a seminar in Australia about dreaming and astral traveling an old aborigine elder approached me. After the seminar, he told me that what I was teaching about astral travel was accurate. He also told me that aborigines have always astral traveled. He said, as a courtesy, when they visited each other astrally they would leave a sprinkling of dust from their area outside the home of the one that they visited. This way those individuals would know they had a nocturnal visitor and they would also know from what region the astral traveler had come. (Evidently, the dust in different areas varies in color and consistency so an aborigine could tell which area a visitor had come from by the dust that he or she left.) This elder, scarred with initiation marks across his chest, stated that he had been going into the prison system to train the young incarcerated aborigine men how to astral travel so "even though their bodies are imprisoned their spirit is free."

Anthropologists, studying various native tribes, find that this journeying with the astral body is a very common event. The cultural beliefs of the astral traveler determine the pattern of that experience. In Eastern Peru, the shaman imagines he is leaving his body in the form of a bird. Asian tribesmen view the silver cord, spoken of by modern metaphysicians, as a ribbon, thread or a rainbow. Africans perceive it as a rope and the natives of Borneo, as a ladder. Regardless of how the term is defined, it nevertheless appears to be a common experience among astral travelers that a type of silver cord remains that serves as a connection between the astral and physical bodies. In your astral dream lover episodes you may notice this silver cord attached to you or your lover.

The scientific view of these dreams is that they are ancestral memories inherited from the days when, according to Darwin's theory, our predecessors were aquatic and airborne creatures. Psychologists refer to it as a type of de-personalization, or a means of avoiding being grounded in normal reality.

Conditions of Travel

In order to program your dream lover excursions for astral meeting, there are three very important conditions to consider. The first is that you believe and appreciate the reality of an astral body, a second body. The second condition is to believe that you can astral travel and specifically focus your desire on leaving your physical body. The third, you must be willing to meet a dream lover in the astral form.

Now, if it were an easy thing to consciously astral travel, it would be an everyday occurrence. However, it is my belief that anyone can experience the existence of an astral body and can have astral dream lovers if the intent is great enough. Astral travel is something that most of us do anyway. We simply don't remember the experience. It can be a frightening experience, when we strongly identify with only our physical bodies rather than our astral. The greatest barrier we encounter is fear itself.

Fear

Even the most "fearless" of us will discover, upon deeper examination, that at some time we have come face to face with the wall of fear. First and foremost, in astral travel, there is the fear of death - the fear that if we are separated from our physical body, perhaps we will die. Our automatic reaction may be to get back within the physical body quickly before we die, that this is where our life is, in the physical. We tend to have these reactions in spite of our emotional attitude and our intellectual thought process. Only after repeating the experience again and again can we hope to release the fear of death. It is much like beginning to swim and eventually realizing that your body <u>will</u> float, that you will not drown.

Another common fear is, "Will I ever be able to get back inside my body?" I can say with absolute certainty that you will always be able to get back into your physical body. There is abundant evidence that those who astral travel are always able to return safely. Fear of the unknown is also faced by many would-be travelers. The healthiest way I know is to work through your fear by simply allowing it to exist and yet be willing to explore the unknown.

Step-by-Step Astral Guide

The following is a step-by-step guide to assist your dream lover astral journeys.

The first step for any astral travel adventures is to put yourself into a deep state of relaxation. (Relaxation can be an acquired skill. To facilitate your relaxation ability you might take stress reduction courses or learn about creative visualizations. You may also try self-hypnosis and use post-hypnotic suggestions Visiting a hypnotist may assist you in setting a post-hypnotic suggestion. Meditation may also facilitate you moving into a very deep state of relaxation.)

After you are in a deep state of relaxation, go even deeper into the space between waking and sleeping consciousness. This is a very delicate balance. You are not yet asleep, but are no longer awake. At this point you might focus on an image or symbol that is unique and special to you. As you move more and more into an even deeper state of relaxation, begin to observe the kind of mind pictures or light patterns that seem to randomly appear. These are sometimes referred to as neural discharges. Do not encourage or deny them. Simply notice them, as you move to an even deeper state of relaxation while maintaining conscious awareness. You will perhaps recognize that you are deepening your consciousness because your body will begin to feel either extremely heavy or very light. Your sense of touch, smell and taste will begin to fade. Occasionally, auditory signals will also begin to fade.

As you are in this very calm, relaxed place, with eyes closed, focus your awareness outside of your body. Begin to imagine you are now at some point outside your body. If it is in another corner of the room, imagine that you are touching the wall. Be aware of the floor and all objects surrounding you. Imagine that you are in this place. Often, as one begins to leave the body, he or she will experience a tingling sensation, or hear a vibration. It is crucial at this point to simply allow the vibrations to increase in frequency. This will occur until the frequency is so high you will almost be unable to perceive it. For some, the body will feel slightly warmer.

The next step is to imagine that you are moving your right or left hand. Imagine yourself reaching out and touching any object that is near. Remember it is not your physical hand, but your astral hand, that is moving.

Another way to enhance this exercise is to imagine touching the wall with your astral hands and then gently pushing against it. Imagine increasing the pressure to a hard push. At one point, it will appear as if your hand or arm is actually going through the wall. Then withdraw your hand.

An excellent technique to astrally meet your dream lover, is to utilize an ancient Etruscan technique. To astral travel the Etruscan's would go into a deep relaxation and then imagine rolling out of their bodies as a means to leave the body. To practice this technique simply lie down; allow yourself to relax, and imagine that you are rolling out of your body. Do this right before bed. Some modern day travelers however prefer a lift-out method where they imagine that they are floating up out of their body. It is important to experiment to discover which method works best for you. Be gentle with yourself. Sometimes, after long periods of practice without attaining any results, in the moment when you least expect it you will experience your first out-of-body journey.

You can also use the Etruscan technique as a way to astrally meet your <u>waking</u> lover. Before sleep, lay side by side your lover. Turn the lights low. Put on some relaxing music. One then imagines rolling into the body of the other one. Breathe and imagine both bodies are merging. Then after several minutes imagine rolling out. Now the other partner imagines rolling in and merging. As you fall asleep side by side, program your dreams for meeting astrally for dream love experiences. (See section on Dream Programming.) As a result of doing the Etruscan technique there will be a very intense energy and psychic connection between you and your partner which will make it easier to meet astrally.

Here are some comments I received about the Etruscan technique and dream lovers.

I was attending Denise Linn's shiatsu seminar and on the third day we were taken through an Etruscan healing exercise. To choose partners, we all bopped around and when the music stopped the person we were closest to was our partner for the exercise. My partner was "Thom" and this was the first time I had noticed him. He was tall, quite good-looking, had dark curly hair and a large, strong, straight nose. But most of all I was impressed with his eyes...brilliant piercing eyes. Very Scorpio I thought. The exercise brought us very close. I find it hard to describe in words. We touched so deeply in that still place within. It seemed to me our spirits connected. When we had finished the exercise, we shared our feelings about how we felt. I remember thinking how Etruscan he looked; almost like a Michaelangelo sculpture. And then we went our separate ways.

Before the close of that day, Denise suggested we program our dreams to create a dream lover. So I did. I dedicated my night to a special lover "with the works" and I asked to recall the dream the next morning.

And did I dream! Into my night fantasy came my Etruscan-looking friend! He seemed so real and so tangible. He had those same bright eyes, the same nose, and the same familiar smile. The place in my dream was like the room where the seminar was held, except it was on another dimension. It was the same, but different. There were people in the room partaking in Denise's seminar in this dream world. Right in the middle of the room I meet my Etruscan friend and we become uninhibited lovers. We make love in every possible way. People are all around paying absolutely no attention to us. They just go about their business, talking to each other, listening to the seminar. They are completely disinterested in our antics. I might add, we were both fully dressed. Yet somehow, this did not seem unusual and did not hinder us. It was an unbelievable experience, immensely pleasurable. I tried to re-create my dream in the next several nights to no avail, yet.

This note was attached to the comments.

Denise, This is all I can remember. It just blew me out!!! I was surprised that the man I did the Etruscan healing with was my Dream Lover. In the exercise I was not aware that I was not physically attracted to him. In fact, I'm not on a conscious level. We obviously connected very strongly during the healing exercise. I do remember feeling that we were one being when we merged. I could feel his heartbeat and his breathing when I rolled into him. The sexual act is another way of rolling in, becoming one, I guess!

The whole experience was incredible for me!!!

Here is another dream that was given me. It seems to be an astral love dream because in the dream she was floating. Floating and flying often occur in astral dreams.

Dear Denise,

My dream occurred about the time I had bought and read the book *Pocketful of Dreams*. I only remember parts of the dream.

There was a beautiful being (male). He was not distinguishable by his features, I only remember him being strong, powerful and very loving. The feeling was a coming together of two souls in total harmony. The experience of love and ecstasy were totally mind-blowing, to the extreme. I remember being aware of totally <u>being</u> there on a bed. As our rhythm built, I could feel an energy flowing through cells in my body as the ecstasy of my partner and myself reached a peak. I found I was floating above the bed. I woke up at that point actually feeling I was floating above my bed. I remember being totally awake at that time.

Carolyn Seeger

Returning to your Body

If you ever wish to return to your body, simply imagine moving either your fingers or your toes in your physical body. This will generally facilitate bringing your spirit back into your body immediately. You can also swallow or move your jaw to bring yourself back. A simple guideline is to activate any one of your five senses.

DREAM LOVERS FROM PAST LIVES

Sarah runs on the rough sea. A vicious wind whips at her thin dress. Cold sleeting rain plasters her long hair to her head. Running. Terrified. A dark specter pursues her through erratic, dark menacing waves. Far away a large cargo ship dances on the tempestuous sea. Knocked back again and again by savage waves, Sarah races toward the ship. Hanging off the side of the ship a rope ladder sways side to side with the violent tossing of the sea. Like a welcome beacon of light, a kind beckoning man in uniform helps her on board. With a deep sigh of relief Sarah nestles in the strong arms of the man that she knows is her lover. The sea calms and delicate rays of sunlight pierce through the clouds as she turns her mouth up to his and tastes the sea on his lips. Looking into the face of the man that had pulled her on board she recognizes the face of her present day husband.

When Sarah told me about this dream, she said she felt that she had seen a glimpse of a past life that she had shared with her present husband. She felt in a past life she and her lover (now her husband) had journeyed by ship to a far away land. She was sure it was a past life memory because it seemed so real and so familiar. In that past life her lover had saved her from being swept overboard by a winter's storm. The past life memories of that storm were interwoven with the dream images. In her present life, she always feels very safe with her husband. Their most enjoyable moments are on their small boat sailing in the sea by their home, though Sarah says she has always had a seemingly irrational fear of storms at sea. (We tend to carry unresolved past life fears from one life to the next.)

Perhaps you've had the eerie experience of dreaming about a foreign town or country that seemed too familiar to describe? Or perhaps you've met someone who seemed very familiar in your dreams, dressed in the clothing of another time in history. As the planet reaches the end of a long cycle and as it increases in momentum, the uncompleted relationships and unfinished business of the past (both in this life and in past lives) will move to the forefront for a long-awaited completion. This increased momentum is causing the mystic veil between this dimension and the next to thin. This thinning will cause past life memories and images to appear in your dreams. Your dreams will increasingly become pathways for you to step through the mystic veil into the past and even meet lovers from the past. In your dreams you can relive and complete old patterns that you have been dragging around with you for lifetimes.

In order to understand past life dream lovers, it is valuable to understand the concept of reincarnation. This idea was present long before recorded history. In fact, it is said that one half of the people in today's world ascribe to the belief of reincarnation. Reincarnation is the idea that the soul is eternal and as such, returns to the earth plane again and again, through rebirth in various bodies, in order to grow and learn. Each lifetime provides a myriad of experiences that allows one, as spirit, to become stronger, more balanced, more loving and eventually, to unite with the all-pervasive spirit known as God.

In one life, you may live in poverty to learn humility and resourcefulness. In another lifetime, you may be extremely wealthy to learn to deal with money fairly and in a positive fashion. In one life, you may be blind in order to learn inner sight, and in another one be athletic, enabling you to experience and fully understand physical strength. You may be a woman in one life and a man in another, or be Caucasian in one and Oriental in another. Past lives are not so much building blocks as they are a jigsaw puzzle with each life contributing to our evolution in being more whole, complete and balanced.

"As ye sow, so shall ye reap." This is the law of karma. Karma is the fate we create for ourselves as a result of our actions in this lifetime as well as in other previous existences. The idea of karma gives an understanding of one may struggle while another has an easy path.

Reincarnation and karma provide us with a clearer picture of our purpose and mission in the present, through our understanding of previous lifetimes. They also give us a better understanding of our destiny in the universe. Life is not a one-time affair nor is it a series of meaningless experiences strung together haphazardly. Rather, it is a mystical on-going journey, that allows you to emerge as a conscious, loving being. The search for your soul may be the most important enterprise you have ever undertaken.

There are volumes of excellent books on the subject for those who are interested in seeking proof of reincarnation. My purpose here, however, is not to refute any doubts regarding past lives, although I firmly believe in them. Rather, I merely intend to illustrate that your dreams and your dream lovers can serve as a doorway to your past. By stepping through that door, you may expand the quality of life beyond your expectations.

To prove beyond reasonable doubt that the images in people's dreams that seem to be from the past are, in fact, actual memories is not nearly as important to me as the results produced when someone spontaneously experiences these past pictures. Altogether too much valuable time has been lost by those who are fearful of being deluded by what otherwise must be acknowledged as an amazing capacity of the human mind.

The value of discovering your past lives is immeasurable. Spiritually exploring past lives and other dimensions are ways to tune into inner guidance. The practice of exploring the distant past leads to personal integration and even to a harmonious unification with the flow of the universe. You find yourself more often in the right place at the right time.

Therapeutically speaking, to release psychological problems without exploring the source beneath surface symptoms is much like attempting to cut weeds with a lawn mower. The problems will re-surface again and again until one dissolves the very roots which created the difficulty. Perhaps someone who compulsively eats may discover that in another life she starved to death and that fear has re-surfaced to create an inappropriate desire for food in this life. By experiencing a past life, either in your waking or dreaming state, you can begin to release past decisions that are still affecting you today.

Children are especially adept at recalling their past lives in the dream state. When my daughter was only eight years old, she shared with me a remarkable dream in which she was a black man in the United States during the time of slavery. She described, in detail, how her pants were ragged at the edges and how she would till the soil with a dilapidated hoe. She confided that some of her present-day friends were also black slaves in that lifetime. Perhaps one of the most curious factors regarding this experience was that one of her friends, whom she had described as being in this dream, unknown to her, had a similar dream wherein she was also a black slave in the deep South of the United States.

In order to connect with your past life lovers during sleep, it becomes important to utilize the variety of techniques described in the section on dream recall. Each evening repeat to yourself before retiring, "Tonight, I dream of a past life lover. Tonight, I dream of a past life lover. Tonight, I dream of a past life lover." Continue to repeat this phrase as you drift off to sleep. When you first begin, you perhaps will find that you only receive a mere wisp of a memory which could be from the past. To receive more clarity with regard to this past life, during your waking hours use your imagination to expand what you have received, regardless of how insignificant it may seem. For example, let's say you saw an ornate helmet in one of your dreams. Upon waking, imagine the kind of lover who might have used that helmet. Imagine where he might have worn it as well as the circumstances surrounding his life. Imagine how you might have felt about this individual. Imagine what the past life relationship could have been. Was it unrequited love or clandestine love or perhaps an enduring marriage? Imagination is an invaluable resource in unwrapping your past. Use your imagination asking yourself, "If I knew, what would this dream lover have been to me in a past life?" and " Does this individual remind me of anyone in my present life?"

Imagine a past life associated with your dream images, and more often than not you will begin to discover who you once were. On many occasions, individuals who have obtained vivid dream past-life experiences have actually travelled to one or more of the places they "remembered" in their dreams. They have then discovered that their dream perceptions were accurate! Past-life recall can be fun in the dream state as well as enormously rewarding during your waking life.

Occasionally a future life lover will appear in your dream. Time is actually circular rather than linear and because of this, future lovers (not only in this life but in future lives as well) will enter your dreams. These future lovers don't always look the same as they will appear in the future but you will recognize him or her by a familiar feeling.

DREAM LOVERS FOR FUN
AND PASSION

Perhaps one of the best reasons for cultivating a dream lover is just for the plain joy and fun of it. Having these nightly encounters can be a tremendous source of ecstasy and happiness. Most people just sleep away their night hours. How wonderful to be able to program your dreams for romance and adventure. One night you can be on the plains of the Wild West holding on tight as you gallop behind a cowboy. Inhaling his very male musky odor, mixed with the scent of fresh hay, you leave a trail of dust to settle in the sunset. The next night you might find yourself eating at the Ritz, alone, when a dark mysterious individual asks to join you. As you sit across from each other, eating silently, this dark stranger's eyes seems to devour you with bite. Each night can offer variety, enjoyment and just plain fun without leaving the comfort of your bedroom or costing a fortune or raising an eyebrow.

Recently, in Bali, on a humid evening, I sat beneath large banana leaves in the flickering torch light as I watched two frogs cavort and hop in frantic play. Their raucous croaking melded with the many exotic night sounds. In that moment I felt a surge of emotion and I began to cry. As the tears rolled down my cheeks I began checking off possible reasons for the tears. No, I wasn't tired. I didn't seem to be suppressing some deep pain or hurt. I was astonished to realize what I was actually experiencing was passion. It was passion! Passion for life! It was the passion of experiencing life totally and in the moment. Passion is a re-awakening. It is a quickening of the life force within us. It is embracing life. It is your connection to spirit and to the natural flow of life. It is your breathing on a crisp mountain morning as you exhale misty ethereal swirls of breath. You can see it in the first ray of red blinding sun exploding over the horizon. You can feel it as a warm ripple through your body as you sink into a candlelight bubble bath. Passion. It moves us to great heights. It expands our creative horizons and allows us to live fully and utterly in the moment. It is an energy as pure and vibrant as the life force that surges through you. Passion does not come from another being. It comes from that deep well within yourself. Passion emanates from your connection to the earth. There is no difference between spiritual passion and sexual passion. They both spring forth from the same source and both transport you beyond inner boundaries.

Your passion can be for the world around you. To some it can be an orgasmic experience to watch a crystal drop of water well up at the end of an icicle to mirror the snow covered landscape. There are those who experience ecstasy upon finding a perfect shell at the sea shore. Passion can be for new ideas and philosophies. It can be an exquisite hunger to learn and understand more.

As a child I owned an old microscope and I used to observe pond water. The excitement and thrill that I experienced was unparalleled as I observed an entire microcosm of life unfold beneath my eyes. Passion can be losing oneself in music, art or poetry. I can remember as a teenager discovering the joys of oil painting. I loved the smell of turpentine and the smooth whiteness of a new canvas. Often I would paint through the night with no thought of weariness or food. Passion can consume you in a new relationship. Often anxiety is confused with passion but in passion, true passion, all of your senses are heightened and there is an expansion of self. Passion is healing. The most powerful passion can be the quest for spirit.

Through creating and deeply experiencing dream lovers, the depth of passion in all areas of your life will begin to expand. As you can embrace lovers within your dreams you will begin to embrace life within your waking hours. You will begin to become turned on to yourself and begin to resonate and vibrate with a powerful life force. Your dream lover can be the key that opens the doors to passion in all areas of your life. Let go and go for it!

CAN DREAM LOVERS INCREASE
YOUR SENSUAL POISE?

Your dream lovers can assist you opening to the rich world of your sensuality. As you have vivid powerful sensual experiences in the night you become much more sensuous in waking life. A sensuous individual is one who intimately experiences and projects a total awareness of all senses. He or she responds and deeply appreciates the sounds, the sights, the tastes, the aromas, and the feel of the environment. Your senses are your doors and windows to the world. They are your way of attuning to the life around you. The more sensitive you become to your senses, the more loving, understanding, enjoying, and deeply sensuous you become. When you look at the truly confident and glowing people around you, most likely one of their vital signs is the intense awareness of their senses. I don't mean in a superficial, hedonistic way, but in a serious, fine-tuned way that allows those individuals to sense all sorts of feelings and facts and awarenesses that others miss. Our senses are complex receiving stations for all life around us, and the more sensitively we attune to our senses, the more sensuous we become.

Most people equate sensuousness with sexuality; and indeed, it is the individual who is in touch with his or her senses that can experience sexuality most fully. For the more totally you can experience another person through your senses, the more total is your union with that being. However, as you expand your senses, not only is your sexuality enhanced, all areas of your life are enhanced. In people who are creative and self-realized, there is a constant reoccurring pattern of delight and skill and sensory experience. Margaret Mead's mother deliberately exposed her daughter to sensory experiences, to different textures and colors, and great works of art, and masterpieces of music. She was encouraged to use her senses in all kinds of activities. When she learned a poem she would enhance her memorization process by vividly seeing in her imagination the images described, as if she was experiencing the textures, the tone, and the feeling of the poem.

Your senses are a gateway to the world; they are keys to unlocking your wellspring of creativity. But cultural and religious denial of our senses has created an uncertain attitude towards cultivating them. Most people in today's world are cut off from their senses, and therefore, cut off from experiencing their world and their life as completely and freely as they can.

As babies, we are sensuous creatures. If our mother touched our toes, our entire body would respond in rapture...our entire body would experience that sense of touch, not just our toes. But as we entered society and school, we began learning 'about' instead of 'with'...and we became distant from our senses. We've become distant from the multi-dimensional, mysterious world of the senses, and have denied ourselves the abundance of reality available through our senses. Allow yourself, within your dreams, to step fully and deeply into the realm of the senses. Often the sights and sounds and smells within your dream can seem even more vivid than in waking life. Relish your senses. Revel in your night time sensual experiences and entire new vistas will open for you in waking life.

Your dream lover can increase your waking sensuality. Here are some suggestions to help you prepare for your night time sensuous adventures.

Preparation for your Sensuous Dream Encounters

1. Take a long warm candlelight bubble bath before bed.
2. After the bath, sensuously massage essential oils into your skin or try lightly dusting powder on your body.
3. Have very sensuous bedding. Toss lots of large, soft down pillows about your bed. Try snuggling into a feather bed. Use flannel, silk, fine cotton or even Italian linen sheets.
4. Light a candle, or two or three, next to your bed, sip port from an elegant goblet and read a romantic novel.
5. Spray your favorite perfume or cologne on yourself and on your pillows.
6. Give yourself a very sensuous massage, gently stroking each part of your body...and allow yourself to enjoy it!
7. Play very sensuous music as you fall asleep.
8. Visualize things that are very sensuous to you. You can use the following exercise for this purpose. You can read this exercise into a tape recorder to play back to yourself while you fall asleep. You might want to

put very sensuous music in the back ground
as you record it.

Sensuality Exercise

*Now is the time to awaken and celebrate your
senses... to encourage and expand your bridges
to your perceptions. To participate in the following exercises, first lie or sit in a comfortable
position, and take three deep full breaths. With
each exhalation, let your body relax. You may do
this now.*

*Now imagine that you are laying on a soft, green
grassy hill, staring up at the clouds on a warm,
early summer afternoon. Feel the warmth of the
ground beneath you. Feel the different areas of
your body that touch the earth. Your heels...the
backs of your legs...your buttocks...your back...the
backs of your arms...the back of your head.
Imagine that you can feel the warmth of the
sunshine on your face as you lay on that soft,
green grassy hill, staring up at the clouds, on a
warm, early summer afternoon. Feel the soft
breeze as it lightly dances across your body.
That's good. Now smell... smell the warm summer air. It smells a little earthy, and slightly like
fresh mown grass. Listen to the drone of the
insects...and the far away sound of a train whistle
as it wafts through the air. Taste the sweetness of
the blade of grass that you have been chewing. It
tastes slightly sweet...and fresh. Now look at the
clouds as they billow and change into endless
fantasies...silhouetted against a deep blue sky.
At any given moment in time, we are saturated in
an ocean of sensory experiences. As you recline
in your imagination, on that grassy hill, let all of*

your sensory perceptions penetrate and fill you. And feel calm, serene, at peace... and totally in touch with your connection with the Universe. You are in harmony with all of life... experiencing totally through, and beyond, your senses.

Now let that scene fade away... just let it fade away.

And now imagine that you are in a canoe in the middle of a lake, on a full moon night. Feel the slight chill in the air. Smell the damp, pungent odor of the lake. Listen to the rhythmic cadence of the paddle as it glides through the water. Look at the dancing reflection of the moon on the lake...and the dramatic outline of the trees against the far shore. Take a minute to completely and totally be aware of the richness of sensory experiences on this full moon boat ride. Make it as real in your imagination as you can. See if you can be aware of all of your senses at once, rather than isolating one sense at a time. You may do this now.

Now, just let that scene fade away...just fade away.

And now imagine that you are sitting by a fireplace, watching images in the crackling flames. Again, allow each of your senses to be totally immersed in this scene. You may do this now. Make it as real as you can.

Let that mental picture also fade away.

And now imagine a scene that has a very pleasurable memory for you. Perhaps it's slipping into freshly ironed, sun-dried sheets... or eating wa-termelon on the Fourth of July... or watching children fly kites in the park... whatever has been a pleasurable memory for you. Remembered pleasures prime your sensorium, and you may find after doing these exercises that your sense awareness will have a keener edge, and your capacity for pleasure will deepen. You may imagine your pleasurable memory now, letting yourself experience the abundance of sensory input within that memory. Make it as real for yourself as possible. You may do this now.

Let that scene drift away.

And finally, wherever you are right now, what-ever position your body is in, center on your experience of the present moment. If your eyes are open, or even if they're closed, what sights are you aware of right now? What are you seeing right now? What sounds are you hearing right now? Listen to the close sounds... hear the far away sounds... even the internal sounds. What can you smell right now? What smells are you aware of? Allow your sense of smell to expand... as you are aware of the smells in your environ-ment right now. Is there a taste that you are experiencing right now? Put your awareness in that part of your body that tastes... and notice what you're tasting right now. And lastly, be aware of the way your body feels right now. If you're laying down, feel where it touches the bed or couch or floor. Allow yourself to feel the temperature of the air against your skin... to be intimately aware of the way your body feels within... to be aware of the surface of your skin, and how your clothes feel against your skin. Now be aware of all your senses at once... experiencing the sights, the sounds, the smell, the taste, and the feeling... that is within you and around you right now. And allow your sense perception to expand. As your sense perception expands, so does your sensuality, your connection to all of life. Your dreams and your dream lovers increase your awareness of your senses and allow you to become more sensuous. You may now fall into a deep sensuous sleep.

Immersing yourself in your sensory experiences before bed will allow you to open the inner door to your sensual nature during your night hours.

HOW TO REMEMBER YOUR DREAM LOVE ENCOUNTERS

The first question that I'm usually asked is,"Gee, it all sounds great, but I just don't remember my dreams, so how am I ever going to have a dream lover?" Dreams are a mysterious language of the night. These nocturnal visions have influenced the destiny of individuals as well as entire nations. Since the dawn of time, our ancestors have looked to their dreams to gain an inner understanding of the outer world. But as a culture, we have forgotten... and dreams have become just relics of our mind. Most people can no longer call upon the Muses of the Night by direct path. We no longer can easily remember our dreams. In our modern culture, it has become commonplace to consider sleeping as a time when we do nothing "productive". Thus, dreams are considered oddities or items of amusement. They are rarely considered valuable or imperative to our well being as are the real events of the day, yet we spend approximately one third of our life asleep.

However, with very little effort, we can regain our ability to tap into our dreams. First, it's important to realize that everyone has dreams. Even those individuals who can only remember a smattering of dreams throughout an entire life time do, indeed, dream. In fact scientists have proved that everyone dreams. Even blind people dream. Young children dream and it is assumed, though not proven, that even infants dream. People with low IQ's have the same number of dreams per night as individuals having high IQ's.

Dreaming is as natural as breathing. There is no way, with the exception of drug use or overindulgence in alcohol, that one can prevent it. So whether or not you remember your dreams, you are definitely dreaming each and every night.

Although it is possible to experience as few as three or as many as nine dreams a night, generally you have an average of four to five dreams a night. In fact, you spend 20 percent of your total sleep time dreaming. You dream, on the average, an hour and a half a night.

Despite very little being known about the mysterious realm of dreams, there are certain physiological changes that occur during REM sleep. (It is generally held that dreams occur when there is rapid eye movement...hence the initials REM.) These physiological changes include the heart rhythm speeding up or slowing down for no accountable reason; the blood pressure climbs to new heights and dives unpredictably; the pulse becomes irregular and breathing can become halting; and spontaneous firing of brain cells are sometime increased beyond normal waking levels.

One physical organ betrays this inner disquietude, however, more than any other . Penile or clitoral engorgement almost always accompanies the dream sleep. In conjunction with this, it is interesting to note that neither wet dreams nor penile erections have ever been documented in dream laboratories. This suggests that with the smallest amount of effort, control of our sleeping states is possible. It also suggests that sexuality and our dreaming states are very closely related.

So you <u>do</u> dream and sexual arousal is a natural component of your dream state. So, how do you remember these dreams that you have so profusely every night? It is an acquired skill that anyone can develop with a moderate amount of effort. The single, most important, element in being able to remember your dreams is <u>motivation</u>. To attain that motivation, you must first perceive your dreams as worthwhile; regard them as valuable messages received from your subconscious. It is imperative that you <u>want</u> to remember your dreams and that you feel that they are important. Know that each dream is a brilliant facet reflecting clear and remarkable insight into the gem that is you. Each dream not only gives you valuable insights about yourself, but each dream and each dream lover can allow for remarkable healing both physically and emotionally.

The attitude that often blocks dream recall is the idea that dreams are un-important. Sometimes, however, there are some other beliefs that will block dream recall. To release these blocks you can program your subconscious mind by repeating an affirmation to yourself to reprogram that attitude. Just repeat the affirmation to yourself again and again (particularly before sleeping). Some useful affirmations to release the limiting beliefs and attitudes around acquiring dream lovers are:

ATTITUDE: I don't feel that dreams are important.

AFFIRMATION: My dreams give me valuable insights into my life that allow for more balance and joy.

ATTITUDE: I'm distressed that I might do something sexually in my dreams that is inconsistent with my waking values.

AFFIRMATION: I do not judge my dreams. I know that every message from my subconscious deserves to be heard.

ATTITUDE: Sexuality in my dreams is disturbing.

AFFIRMATION: I deserve sexual pleasure and it's enjoyable to experience dream sex.

ATTITUDE: I'm not really sure I actually want to know what is in my subconscious.

AFFIRMATION: My dreams give me valuable perceptions into my life that allow for more balance and joy.

ATTITUDE: I am afraid that if I have dream lovers, it will negatively affect my relationship.

AFFIRMATION: My relationship is greatly enhanced by all activities in my dreams. All my relationships are improved by my willingness to delve into my sensual nature.

ATTITUDE: I need sleep. Dreaming about dream lovers might interrupt my being able to get a good night's sleep.

AFFIRMATION: I get all the sleep that I need. Connecting with dream lovers fills my waking hours with energy.

Your Dream Journal

Most dreams are forgotten within ten minutes. Dream research has revealed that when a dreamer is awakened during rapid eye movement (REM) sleep, the subject recounts being right in the middle of a dream. Awakened immediately after REM sleep, he or she recalls a completed dream. Five minutes after REM sleep, sleepers remember only fragments of dreams. Ten minutes after REM sleep, there is no recall at all. Thus it is only during the few moments immediately after dreaming that a dream is still vivid and in your mind. For this reason it is imperative that you record your dream immediately upon waking while it is fresh in your memory. Even if you are sure that you will remember your dream, often in morning's light, it is lost. Write it down immediately (or tape record) as much detail as you can.

To Record Your Dreams You Will Need:

1. An easy flowing pen.
2. Notebook, journal or tape recorder, preferably a Dictaphone.
3. Flashlight or night light (if using a notebook).

An easy way to record your dreams is to purchase a pen with its own light. These can be bought at medical supply stores. Or a less costly way to accomplish this is to purchase a penlight and strap it to your pen.

It is beneficial to divide your dream journal into two sections. One for the dream recall and one for the interpretation and the realizations that flow from that dream. You also might want to record the date of the dream and what is occurring in your life at the time. Also, recording the date can allow for a later realization concerning a particular dream on a particular date. For example, you may have had a powerful dream on January 11th and then later realized that that was your parents' wedding anniversary. While not being consciously aware of it at the time, nevertheless, your mind was responding to the emotions and feelings you have in regard to your parent's relationship. Later, having this information may provide you with clues and valuable insights regarding yourself and your own relationships.

When recording your dream, also note the feelings that occur in the dream. It is essential that you write down your memories quickly because, literally, in seconds the dream will begin to fade. Jot down predominant colors, symbols, key words, themes and emotions. Try not to get stuck on some detail to the detriment of recording the rest of the dream. If you heard a poem or an interesting verbal expression or phrase, record that data first. Later record the visual parts you remember. The visual images tend to be retained longer than auditory stimuli, so it is a good idea to first record anything you <u>heard</u>.

For individuals who find it difficult to come to enough conscious awareness to turn on a flashlight or a tape recorder, there is an *eyes-closed technique* you can use. As you awaken, feel for the notebook that is next to your bed. Then, with your eyes still closed so that you are allowing yourself to be very much involved in your dream state, begin to write. You will have to experiment with finding a way to keep from writing over what you have already written. One method of avoiding superimposing writing is to extend the little finger of the writing hand as a guide in finding the edge of the paper; this gives you some definition of where you are. You can either use it as guide on the top of the page or on the side of the page. As I have difficulty reading my own handwriting when I'm fully awake, this is not the best technique for me. I awaken to unintelligible scribbles that give me no clue whatsoever as to the night's drama. Nevertheless, some find this technique valuable, so I have included it for this reason. Later, you will need to transfer what you have written onto a two-sided notebook so that you can write your interpretation beside it.

Tape Recorder

The advantage of a tape recorder is that you can usually stay in a deeper brain level and thus stay more in touch with those vivid dream images than when you are writing your dream down. For those who have a hard time going back to sleep after writing down a dream, a tape recorder (voice activated is best) is an excellent tool. It can enable you to record more detail in less time than if you are writing. A disadvantage to using a tape recorder is that you will later need to transcribe the dream if you are going to keep a running record of your dream progress. Another disadvantage is that often, in the night, it may seem that you are communicating clearly, but you can be dismayed to find in the morning that you are not able to understand your midnight ramblings. Very often your voice will sound as if you have come from another dimension and, in fact, you have. If you are not using a voice activated model, you might consider getting the small hand-held type that is used for dictation. These are easier to use in the dark than the larger models.

Flashlight

A flashlight is necessary if you are recording in a journal. The small battery-operated lanterns (not hand-held) sold in camping supply shops seem to work the best. Using one of these will keep you from having to juggle the flashlight as you try to write.

To begin to record your dreams:

- Put your tape recorder or journal next to your bed with flashlight and pen and visible clock.

- Lie in a position that allows your spine to be straight while you program yourself for dream recall.

- Choose one of the "Before Sleep Techniques".

Techniques to Help Remember your Dreams

Tibetan Dream Meditation

As you lay down to go to sleep, <u>intently concentrate on your desire for dream recall</u>. Now focus that intention as if it were in the back of your throat. You might imagine a glowing blue sphere in the throat area and within that blue orb imagine putting your desire for dream recall. Hold that visualization until you fall asleep. Using this technique, you may find that your dream recall is greatly increased. It is interesting to note that this ancient Tibetan technique has an interesting physiological parallel. Research has shown that it is this very area in the back of the throat (the stem of the brain) which controls the activation during dream states. Thus, by connecting with this potent area before sleep, we are beginning the stimulation of dream activity and dream recall.

Water Technique

Drink half of a full glass of water before retiring and, as you are drinking this water, affirm to yourself, **"Tonight I remember my dreams."** Upon waking in the morning, if no dream recall is evident, drink the remaining half of the glass of water, saying to yourself, **"My dreams are recalled, now and through the day."** Very often drinking the second half of the glass of water stimulates dream recall. Sometimes that recall will occur spontaneously during the day.

Third Eye Technique

This is another technique using water for remembering your dreams. Put a bowl of water next to your bed. Right before sleep, dip two fingers into the water and lightly touch your throat. Then rub these two fingers on your forehead in the area of your third eye (the area between and slightly above your eyes). As you rub this area, affirm recalling your dreams. The next morning again touch these two areas with water. Very often this will stimulate recall.

Spiritual Assistance

Relax your body with your spine straight. Let your mind become still and receptive. Pray to God or ask your dream guide for assistance in remembering your dreams. Strongly affirm that you *will* remember your dreams and repeat this to yourself several times before falling asleep.

Creative Visualization

As you begin to fall asleep, visualize yourself waking up, looking at the clock, noting the time and intently writing down a dream. Then, continue this visualization forward in time until you are seeing yourself waking in the morning and writing down another dream. Visualize yourself looking and feeling very satisfied because you have successfully recorded your dreams.

Aromatherapy

Research has shown that, of all the senses, the one sense which we use as the most powerful criteria to be attracted or repelled by someone, is the sense of smell. It is not so much the way someone looks or the way they sound but, surprisingly, it is the way they smell. The sense of smell can be used as a powerful technique to remember your dreams. For aromatherapy you can use incense or mix a small amount of essential oil (such as a mixture of sandalwood for spirituality and ylang ylang for sensuality) and water together and place in a small bowl. Beneath this bowl place a small flame. This will create a lovely aroma in the room. (Many gift stores carry ceramic-type vases specifically for aromatherapy,) With your hands imagine that you are cupping some of this smell and imagine you are pouring the aroma over yourself as a purification ritual. As you do this say to yourself **"Tonight I remember my dreams!! Tonight I remember my dreams!"** When you enter the area where you will sleep, burn the herbs sage, cedar, juniper or sweet grasses. This native American smoke ritual is an ancient method of dedication and purification. The smoke of those herbs is thought to have a purifying effect and be a direct communion with Spirit. It is felt that one's prayers go up through the smoke and Spirit sends prayers down through the smoke. Through your prayers you can ask for a spiritual dream love experience. Here is a step-by-step technique you might consider using.

- As you are in bed, say a prayer giving thanks for the goodness in each day and affirm your intention to live a balanced and compassionate life.

- Then imagine a double helix of upward spiraling energy spinning through you affirming you will remember your dream lover. Your very last thoughts before sleep are the thoughts that very often will affect your dreams.

- Give thanks in the morning for all that you have received, whatever it might be.

Morning Dream Recall
Rolling

Research has shown that dreamers will usually roll over or change positions immediately after a dream. It is thought that this assists the brain to move into a different brain wave pattern. Be still when you first awake. When you write in your dream journal, after a dream, try to move as little as possible. Dream research has shown that movement very often will impair recall. It has been found, in dream laboratories, when people roll over as they are awakened from a dream, they have a more difficult time remembering their dream. If you didn't recall your dreams, roll into a new position. Sometimes this will spontaneously generate dream images. The dream is coded into the position that you were in, while you had it, and a gentle rolling can initiate recall. Use the Rolling Technique only if there *isn't* any dream memory.

Conversation

Immediately after waking up share with someone about what you remember. Just beginning to talk about your dream will allow more of it to rise to your consciousness.

Writing

When you write your dream in your dream journal, just write whatever you remember, even if it's only a word or a feeling. Even if it's only a dream fragment, record it. It can be an important missing link for self-understanding. If you don't remember, then write the words, "I don't remember my dream", and very often this will stimulate dream recall. Or write down what your feeling is about <u>not</u> remembering and often this is a clue to memory. No matter how sure you are that you will remember the dream, you most probably will not. Write it down. Record each dream as it occurs. It is difficult to record all your dreams in the morning. Laboratory tests have shown that even if someone does remember all their dreams in the morning, they are less vivid and detailed than if they are recorded individually as they occur. Just imagine watching four or five movies over an eight-hour period and then trying to remember them all at one time. Your memory is more exact if you remember and record them as they occur.

Nightmares!

Write down all your dreams, even nightmares and dreams that you <u>don't</u> feel good about, not just the "good" dreams. We are not just "good." We are whole...a balance of light and dark, yin and yang, "good" and "bad." We are total infinite beings. It is important to honor and accept all aspects of ourselves. Each dream is important. As you write your dream down remind yourself that this dream is <u>indeed</u> important.

Gestalt

Put out two pillows. Sit on one and say to the other. "O.K., dreams, why aren't you coming into my memory?" Then move to the other pillow and answer. An example would be, "You are always in such a rush in the morning I never feel that I have the time to come forward." Move back and forth between each cushion as the dialogue continues. Notice the different voices and body postures for the two pillow positions.

This exercise can be done in writing as well.

Mood savoring

So you didn't remember your dream? With your eyes still closed, while you are in bed, notice the mood you are in. Savor that mood like you would a fine wine. Indulge in that mood. Make it more. When was the last time that you felt this exact mood? Often the last time you felt that same mood is a key to your dream. The emotion often keys the mind into dream memory.

Flash!

Often a dream doesn't appear but we will have a vague feeling that a dream is just around the corner of our mind. It is as if it is delicately perched on the edge of our consciousness waiting for some familiar element in our waking life to stimulate recall. These images can be so fleeting that it takes being subtly conscious of the images that suddenly pop into our mind. Watch those images that flash into your mind during the day.

Naps!

Sleep for shorter periods but sleep two or three times a day. If you can change your sleeping patterns so that you have five hours of sleep at night and then one or two naps you will feel more refreshed because you are constantly refreshing yourself and you will recall your dreams much more easily.

Study about Dreams
Study as much as you can about dreams. Where intention goes energy flows, and as you increase your awareness in the area of dreams you will increase dream recall.

Wake up naturally
Train yourself to wake up before your alarm. It's much easier to remember dreams if you waken naturally. Waking up to an alarm often alters the quality of your dream.

Still can't remember?
If you are still not remembering your dreams, find a way to sleep more lightly. Drink a lot of water before bed so you'll have to get up during the night to go to the bathroom. Sleep in a chair. Any way that you can figure out to sleep lightly contributes to your dream recall.

You can also imagine that it is the night before and you are getting ready for bed, brushing your teeth, lying down and going to sleep. Then allow yourself to just watch the images and feelings that occur...use your imagination. (Where do you think imagination comes from anyway?)

If you still don't remember your dream, begin to doodle. Just begin simply doodling in your dream journal. Very often this triggers associations and sparks your memory.

Guilt?
Don't feel guilty if you didn't remember a dream. Guilt will only hinder your future progress. And if you do feel guilty, don't feel guilty about feeling guilty.

Fun!!!!

You don't have to recall all your dreams. If you don't feel like it...don't do it. Dream recall and recording should be fun!

PROGRAM YOUR DREAMS

Programming your dreams is the concept that one can consciously guide the course of dreams from the waking state. Not only can you program for a dream lover, you can program your dreams for many things. For example, a problem presented during waking hours can be resolved during sleeping hours, simply by making a conscious choice to do so. You have perhaps heard the expression "sleep on it", which refers to programming your dreams for problem solving. Sometimes, seemingly putting the problem in the background and getting a good night's sleep can lead to a solution or a resolution through a dream. Developing this communication with your dreams can give you answers to many questions in your life.

Perhaps you need information about a career move. You can literally program your dreams much like you can program a computer. Before you go to bed simply say to yourself, "Dreams, what would be a valuable career move for me?" Or, "I need information with regard to my weight. Why am I having difficulty losing weight, and what can I do to assist myself in this situation?" Or, "Dreams, I have not been feeling well lately. Is there any specific nutritional guidance which will facilitate me in creating good health?" Each of these is an example of dream programming. You can even inquire about dreams experienced the previous night with regard to specific understanding. "Dreams, why couldn't I see my dream lover's face in my dream last night? What was the meaning of that dream?"

Almost everyone who studies dreams concurs that they allow us to get in touch with hidden parts of ourselves, tapping wisdom far greater than anything we are aware of on the plane of normal consciousness. It is the goal of us, the dream makers, to translate these non-physical, non-material expressions into images that make sense in our three-dimensional, linear consciousness. The goal in dream incubating is to be able to create a dream that makes as much sense as possible, that is very clear and understandable. Hence, a dream that demonstrates the value of dream programming.

One can also program dreams for the purpose of testing possible future relationships. By imagining possible conclusions, one can examine future actions as well as compute the outcomes. This enables one to experience an outcome without actually taking the relationship to its completion in waking life.

When you incubate for dream lovers, it is often likely that you will experience profound emotions in the dream state and in waking life. Enjoy your emotions as you would enjoy a symphony. Be willing to experience the full gamut of your emotions. Allow your feelings to ride the waves of the high and low periods that present themselves to you. Breathe in the excitement when listening to the crescendo and decrescendo of your own majestic symphony. Enjoy the anger, caress the sadness, experience the boredom, celebrate each nuance and variation as they occur. Enjoy all aspects of your dreams, including the humiliation, the fear, and the anger. Each is an integral thread in the weaving of life.

One can even program dream lovers simply for the enjoyment of it just as you would experience a first-run movie, a video or a favorite television show. You can program dreams just for the fun of it! They do not always need to be scrutinized for the significant meaning in your life.

Here are some simple guidelines that will help insure success for programming your dreams for dream lovers:

1. Choose a time when you are not too tired. Make certain you will have plenty of time in the morning to process the information given during the night. Choose a time when you have had no drugs or alcohol.

2. If there is an area that you want to program first begin to contemplate the specific area. Do you want to gain a past-life Dream Lover? Do you want to gain a Dream Lover to help with physical healing? Do you want to dream share? Do you want your Dream Lover experiences to help your marriage? Consider the solutions already presented, get in touch with the feelings and emotions you have concerning this specific area with which you want to work. Weigh what you may need to release if you are to gain immediate results. Ask yourself, "Am I willing to have results in this area?" or "Am I willing to let go of this difficulty?" Consider how different life may be if you gained what you desire regarding your Dream Lover. Once you have evaluated the issues

from the perspective of your emotions, your thoughts, your attitudes, perhaps even body sensations, then say to yourself firmly and with conviction, "Tonight I have a Dream Lover experience that allows me much greater communication skills in my waking life." or "Tonight I meet my Dream Lover and gain greater spiritual understanding as a result of that union." That is an affirmation. You are affirming your desire to gain a Dream Lover. Further suggestions for some affirmations you can use, are in the section on programming your dreams according to the phases of the moon.

3. Place your journal or your tape recorder beside your bed. Make sure your spine is straight. As you fall into a deep sleep, repeat your request several times. As you are falling asleep, imagine that you are releasing all the thoughts, attitudes and feelings you have had regarding that area you want to work with. Simply concentrate on your affirmation, repeating it over and over to yourself. If you notice any distracting thoughts, simply allow them to filter in and out of your awareness, always returning to your question. "Dreams, bring me a dream lover tonight. Tonight, I experience deep love and acceptance of myself." Hold such thoughts as these in your mind until you drift off to sleep.

4. And now, simply fall asleep. Programmed dreams usually occur the very same night you have requested them. Occasionally, they will occur the following night. Trust any information that is revealed whether or not it appears

to make sense at the time. Write any items received immediately upon waking. Be patient in waiting for the understanding. Frequently it is not until the following day or even the next week that you are able to make any association between that dream and the issue from which it was programmed. Any programming efforts which you perceived as failures often, in fact, prove to be quite valuable. Go ahead...trust that there is a higher part of yourself that is assisting you in your dreams.

The idea of programing dreams (or dream incubation as it is sometimes called) originated in ancient Greece. Research indicates that there were 300 to 400 temples built in honor of the god Asclepius. These temples were in active use for nearly 1000 years, beginning at the end of the sixth century B.C. and culminating with the end of the fifth century A.D. Dreamers would go to a sacred place, the dream temple, to sleep for the purpose of receiving a useful dream from a god. There was the belief that by sleeping in holy places and appealing to a god, they could obtain profound answers to their inner questions. To participate in modern day dream incubation, it is not necessary to sleep in a sacred place nor appeal to a specific god. However, I do find that if I honor my place of sleep as an inner temple, and if I appeal to Spirit, this assists me in both the vivid clarity and the contents of my dream incubation. If possible, locate a beautiful place in nature as was done in ancient times and create a sacred sleeping chamber. Call upon the Great Spirit, God or even your Guide to lead you through the night hours asking for the dream lover you desire. Ancient Indians, Chinese,

Japanese, Egyptians, Hebrews, and Moslems all practiced dream incubation in places of the rare beauty found in nature.

With regard to programming your dreams, anticipate having all your dream expectations met. In ancient times, the dreamer would participate in purification rites, sacrifices, rituals and ceremonies. However, the same effect can be produced if you have a clear intention when you program your dream. The manner in which you phrase your dream programming statement is very important. Instead of, "I hope that tonight I can locate a dream lover," say, "Tonight, I have a dream lover." Your dreams will respond in clarity proportionately to your intention.

SOME SUGGESTED AREAS TO PROGRAM YOUR DREAM LOVERS FOR:

- Physical healing
- Past-life
- Spiritual experiences
- Sexual healing
- Astral traveling
- Dream sharing
- Soulmates
- Increase passion
- Just plain fun!!!

Programming for a Dream Lover-A Meditation

Here is a guided meditation that you can record for yourself on tape to play before bed. It will help program your night hours for dream love

experiences. (You can also read this meditation
to a friend or lover before bed.) To begin first
create a restful setting...phone off the hook and
lights low. Be in a setting where you will have
little or no distraction. Use a very slow, sensuous
voice when doing this meditation. If you are
making a tape, you may wish to have some music
in the background. Select music that is very
sensuous and arousing for you.

*To begin this dream lover meditation, first make certain
that your body is completely comfortable and in a
relaxed position. Good. Now, check to see that your
spine is straight and your arms and legs uncrossed.
That's good. Your body now begins to move into very
deep relaxation. Each breath you take allows you to
move deeper and deeper within yourself. Simply watch
your breath for a moment. You aren't encouraging your
breath or denying your breath, just observing your breath.
Each breath is allowing you to become more and more
relaxed.   In and out...day and night...light and
dark...black and white...male and female...yin and yang.
There are two opposing, yet complementary, forces exist-
ing in the universe. In this moment, you are aligning and
becoming one with those forces. In and out...keep
watching your breath. Good. Now allow each breath to
become deeper and fuller, deeper and fuller. Nice, deep,
full breaths. That's good. Counting from ten to one with
each number you let go even more... relax even more.
Ten...nine...eight...seven...relaxing   more   and
more...six...five...four... letting go more and more with
each number...three...two...one. You are now completely
relaxed. It feels good to be so very relaxed.*

*Now allow your imagination to take wing and see
yourself in an enchanted, moonlit meadow. The moon is
spilling out of the heavens in cascading waterfalls of*

light. A mist of scented jasmine caresses the slumbering ferns already curled up for the night. A dream owl hovers overhead, his silvery reflection in the stream below seen only by the stars. The surrounding trees murmur gentle secrets in their soft-footed shadows.

There is a quiet magic in the air.

Now spend some time imagining yourself in this secret garden of the night. Make it as real as you can. Imagine yourself using all of your senses to experience this place of quiet beauty, and imagine yourself walking through the meadow. If you cannot visualize, get a sense or a feeling of being in the meadow. Your body feels very graceful, very sensuous, very relaxed and easy.

You notice that in the center of the meadow there is a bed. It is a sumptuous bed. It is so luxurious and voluptuous. The pillows are soft and round and firm. Take some time to really imagine this bed, making it as real as possible. Make it your perfect bed. It might be a big, four-poster bed like your grandmother's feather bed or, perhaps, a canopied bed draped with gossamer, luminescent fabric lightly caressed by the warm breeze. What kind of bed is this? Really imagine this bed.

Now slowly and ever so sensuously, climb into this bed. Be aware of the opulent plumpness of the pillows. Feel the silky smoothness of the sheets as you slide easily beneath the covers. It feels so good to be in this bed. Fanned by the gentle fragrance of the night, you find yourself drifting off into a deep, deep, deep sleep. Deep....deep.....deep.........sleeeeeep.

Somewhere in the magic of the night, you gently roll over and stretch. As you do, your hand brushes against a warm body. Your eyes are closed, yet you intuitively know this is your dream lover. While you tentatively explore the subtle curves in the mountains and valleys of your lover's body, twilight dances on your silhouettes and the entire heavens are a part of you. Deliciously warm waves of intimacy bathe your being. You caress and possess, and experience the faint, stirring breath of your dream lover softly in your hair. Take just a few moments to imagine the most exquisite...the most remarkable love-making. Feel your spirit, your entire being, soar to unlimited heights.

The dawn is approaching. As you lie nestled in your lover's arms, feeling such a lingering sense of deep fulfillment, you drift off into a contented sleep. When your eyes open, the sunlight is sending yellow needles darting through the joyous spaces of the forest trees. Your dream lover has vanished in the silent whispers of the night. A perfect rose graces your pillow.

At the end of this meditation, you can either move into the sleep state or move to normal waking consciousness. If you wish to return to normal waking consciousness, then count from one to ten and suggest that with each number, you feel more and more awake.

USE THE MOON TO FIND YOUR DREAM LOVER

Moon energy can open the inner door to the garden of dream lovers. The moon is one of the most potent keys to the inner realms where your dream lover resides.

The moon is the silvery white goddess, illuminator of the unconscious, revealer of mysterious forces. She journeys silently into the night, emissary from the land of dreams. She is the giver of visions and allows you to see deep within to the wellspring of all love and lovers. All tides are hers. Tides of the great seas...tides of the sky...tides of the inner realms of the night. She is a celestial goddess of dreams. She carries the moon tides gently to the center of the soul...tides that ebb and flow. All these secrets belong to her.

The moon rules the great deep where all life began. She is the mistress of the inner tides that never cease. She is ruler of fantasies and intuition. She brings creativity and vision on the dream tides of the night.

Sleep and darkness are her gentle companions. She returns month after month with renewed strength. She unites opposing elements, transforming darkness into light. She is the source of all physical and spiritual rebirth and illumination. She cascades from the doorways of heaven in waterfalls of light. She is the moon...a powerful spiritual force on our planet and ruler of the dream tides that ebb and flow in the night.

Moon consciousness or moon awareness arises from the deep core of our being; it is inherent within our internal instincts. To primitive people, the moon was a visible and revered symbol of our inner states of dreaming. Today, the moon touches a memory of the forgotten arts, one of which is to recall and understand our dreams. Ancient civilizations honored the moon for it played an important part in their everyday lives. They observed how crops grew seasonally and in tune with the cycles of the moon. A woman's menstrual cycle synchronized with lunar rhythms. The moon was the ultimate symbol of fertility in the universe; her gentle light dew moistened the plants after the heat of the day. The light of the moon invited life to come forth from the seeds during the night. With the same mystical force, it drew plants from the earth, the monthly bleeding from women, and tides to and from the shore. It was the bearer of wisdom in the night through dreams.

The moon was necessary to all of life, and her cycles imperative in all fertility. In past times, an important relationship was acknowledged between one's dreams and one's daily life. Since night, the special dominion of the moon, brought sleep and visions, dreams were revered as messages from the moon to be carefully followed the next day. The moon was believed to be the originator of all creativity.

Early civilizations observed that being in or out of sync with the rhythms of the moon would influence their health and balance. These people measured all life by the lunar cycles. Activities from planting crops to cutting hair to engaging in battle were all acknowledged to be more successful when done in alignment with the moon cycles.

One of the most basic aspects of our existence is our bodily cycles. These internal flows seem to define the very way we experience ourselves and the world around us. The moon is a major regulator of many of these individual rhythms. The moon affects the tides on the surface of the earth, and even slightly distorts the earth in its direction. This cyclical pull dramatically affects our body fluids as well as our dream states. Since the body is 98 percent water, and in view of the fact that our blood has a chemistry very similar to sea water, it is easy to understand how our dream states and body changes synchronize with the ocean tides and phases of the moon.

An intimate knowledge of and exposure to the moon can increase one's inner knowing. A mastery of inner dream states can be acquired by understanding and aligning with moon cycles. All life is cyclical. Developing awareness of moon cycles, as well as our own life cycles, will provide us with greater insight into our dreams. To maximize our understanding and interpretation of our dreams, it is of paramount importance to create our own alignment with the moon and its cycles.

One of the universal principles learned from lunar cycles by ancient peoples was the basic pattern for renewal. Rest, meditation and gestation were treated with the same reverence as productivity. The understanding of equal respect for all parts of the cycle has been most clearly retained in the Oriental concept of yin and yang and its adherence to the cosmic laws of balance.

Each cycle of the moon is divided into four smaller cycles: new moon, waxing moon, full moon and waning moon. Each cycle is about seven days in length. There are no set moments when one cycle ends, and another begins. They simply follow a flow pattern as does our own physical energy.

The new moon is the time of rebirth. During this time, rest, be still, meditate. Dreams occurring during this time reflect the deepest and most internal movements of your inner self. This was a time when ancient American Indians sought retreat in nature in order to be still and to commune with Great Spirit. In the midst of this stillness, your dreams are preparing the soil of your inner soul for the planting of seeds in the weeks to come.

As the crescent moon appears, be aware as your energy begins to expand. When the moon waxes or enlarges, begin to take action in alignment with the revelations you received in your dreams during the new moon.

The full moon is the culmination of the seed planted in the new moon. During this cycle, release the fullness of your creative forces. Be alive and animated. Participate fully in life and enjoy the dance of celebration. Research indicates this is the cycle when the most vivid dream activity occurs. This is also the time when you are most likely to recall your dreams, and the number of dreams you experience will also increase during the full moon.

The waning moon is a time to assimilate and absorb all you have learned in previous weeks. The dreams during this time will be dreams of reflection and introspection. When you begin to integrate your life movements with the moon's cycles, you will be flowing in harmony with the most primordial and powerful force in nature. Your dream life will become increasingly vivid and viable.

One way to integrate life cycles with those of the moon is to create a moon ritual. In ancient moon rituals, visions, whimsy and intuition were all valued as absolute necessities in the rationale of living. In fact, without these states, it was thought that a balance of life was not possible, and that one's understanding of the universe dwindled. It is essential to our own individual and collective balance to regain an understanding of these states of being. This can be achieved by creating a moon ritual for oneself.

A moon ritual is the channeling of energies of the universe, utilizing the moon as a focal point, in order to usher oneself into more expanded levels of consciousness. All mysteries and powers of the subconscious are symbolized by a moon ritual. It is that elusive quality with which the moon priestess of old would desire to merge.

A ritual can be used to change one's perceptions of reality. It is a symbolic event. It can either be simple or complex in nature. The ritual attempts to make tangible an event which has occurred on the inner plane. A transformation of personality is implied in every ritual. It is a means to experience connectedness with the entire universe.

Here are some simple modern-day moon rituals that you can use to enhance your dreaming hours:

• Stand at a window or be outdoors during the different phases of the moon.

• Lift your arms to the moon as ancient people have done before you. Feel the energy of the moon surge and fill every cell of your being.

• Take a moon bath and allow the light rays of the moon to bathe and cleanse you, washing over the deepest parts of you like waves of the sea.

• Dance in the light of the moon. Allow yourself to move with wild abandon.

• Leave water out in the light of the moon and just before you go to sleep, drink this water which has been energized from the deepest well- spring of life.

A ritual is a stylized series of actions used to bring about change. It has its origin deep in the psyche of each individual. Therefore, you already possess within you the ingredients from your own unconscious to trigger all the experiences you desire. So, look within and create a moon ritual that speaks to your life and your needs using symbols and artifacts that are representations for you of the inner qualities of dreams.

The Dream Lover Moon Ritual I have created for myself is simple. I lay out a circle with sticks or special stones. The circle represents wholeness and my inner dream world. Without beginning or end, it represents the cycle of the universe, the source and eventual return to the source. I use a circle to represent the moon and my dreams, the source of life and unity. Within this circle, I place things that represent the mystical world of dreams and things that represent love in my dreams. Among these is the stone, selenite, a name originating from the Moon Goddess, Selene. This stone is an excellent tool in assisting dream recall and dream understanding as well as being excellent to program for dream love experiences.

To enhance the ceremonial aspect of my own moon circle, I begin by dedicating my energy to the living spirit in all things and to my Dream Lovers. I then compose a simple dream song and create a dream dance that will invoke the power of life and my own inner nature. Once I have completed my ritual, I carefully gather the treasured objects I have used in my ritual and place them in a special location until my next moon ritual.

When you first create your own moon ritual and begin to participate in it, it is not unusual for you to experience feelings of foolishness or awkwardness. However, as you persist beyond that point of feeling foolish, you will soon experience the sacred center. At the beginning of the ritual, your true emotions are buried under layers of linear and rational thinking. Yet, as you persist, the right side of your brain, the Isis side, will take over and the inner reality of the acts performed will come through. As a result, you will feel yourself walking in harmony with the inner cycles of nature and in harmony with your dreams and the inner sages of the night.

A Moon Month of Affirmations for Dream Lovers

Listed on the following pages are affirmations. They are meant to be used nightly for 28 days. They are designed to coincide with the phases of the moon. Attuning yourself with the cycles of the moon will add more potency to your dreams.

The lunar rhythm cycle compares to the cycle of making love. There are four phases of the moon (as explained in the previous section). The first seven days are known as the waxing. This is the first stage of development. The first two nights the new moon is not visible. The third and fourth night a form is emerging in the shape of a thin crescent. This heralds the beginnings of something exciting and mysterious. A percentage of the moon is not yet visible. It is hidden and concealed. So it is when we meet someone to whom we are attracted. The magic begins, yet there is a part of us that holds back and we conceal our true feelings in our hearts for fear of rejection. We hide behind a shield until we can begin to feel more secure with that other person.

Slowly, as the relationship develops, we grow more trusting and we open our hearts to disclose intimate information. The new moon may be likened to foreplay, an exciting yet gentle unfolding. Along this path there may be discomfort, insecurity, fear and timidity. Trust the process, allow the chrysalis of the soul to germinate and wax.

As the moon expands so will your dreams. The experiences with your dream lover become vivid and active. This is an important time to ask your dream partner to come to you in the night, so you can experience passionate, enlightening, sensuous adventures. Similarly, as the moon increases, so the energy in lovemaking escalates and moon fluids flow.

As the full moon reaches its zenith, the culmination of the lovemaking reaches a crescendo. This is the moment when you can integrate with the energy of the Universe, transcend into higher consciousness and know that you are harmonizing with nature and the Moon Goddess.

The feelings and emotions experienced after lovemaking allow for feelings of love, compassion and a deepening connection to your lover. These blissful waves of ecstasy wash through your body revitalizing and balancing you. Just as the waning moon assimilates and absorbs energy, so your body engages in a renewal of energy. It is also a time for pulling your energy inward and reflecting on what has occurred. The content of your dreams at this time may have a profound quality which offers you a deeper understanding of your life's destiny. The waning moon is a time for healing. In the aftermath of lovemaking, a pathway becomes clear to heart and soul, allowing love to flow. As the passion wanes, the body becomes still. Peace and harmony couple together and the creative force begins to birth. As the crescent moon retreats, Dream Lovers provide the opportunity for you to become aligned to a higher consciousness. The yearning for unfolding mystical and magical secrets continues. A new moon births, a new dream lover enters.

You are now ready for that night to begin.

Repeat the appropriate affirmation to yourself again and again as you go to sleep. If you are unsure where to start, check a calendar for the dates of the full and new moon. You can start anywhere, just make sure your affirmations are in sync with the moon cycles. For example, if it is a night of a full moon go to the page that shows the full moon and do that affirmation for that night and continue from that point for the following nights.

(Thanks to Patricia Nugent for her assistance with this section.)

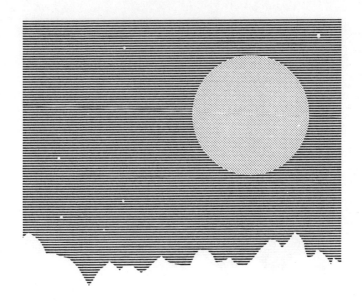

I am willing and open to receive and experience a
dream lover.

Sexual energy is innocent. It is our past
conditioning that traps us into feeling guilty and
thinking that sex is sinful. Be ready to experience
sexual energy. Know it is all part of the
Universal Life Force. Your dream lover
connects you to Spirit. Be trusting of the process.

*In the dark stillness, I allow the mystical wonder of a
dream lover to embrace me.*

Use this affirmation to help program the
subconscious mind to invite a dream lover into
your night-time adventures. It helps create a
safe space for this connection. Before you fall
asleep visualize the sort of Dream Lover with
whom you would like to connect. In the still
darkness of the night listen to your own
heartbeat. Know that this mysterious
rendezvous is inviting a deeper connection with
your higher self. It is a safe, yet mystical
process.

I accept and appreciate my body. I deserve love.

The most important message your Higher Self
communicates to you is "Love yourself."
Before bed, look in a full-length mirror and
love and appreciate what you see. Rejoice!
Your body is a divine form created by God.
Each tiny cell is a masterpiece of craftsmanship,
a constant vehicle refurbishing itself.
Acknowledge this gift and see the beauty in
yourself. Ask your Dream Lover to help you
fully appreciate your body and express your
beauty more and more each day.

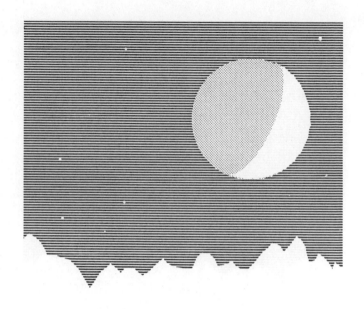

I am safe as I open to my sexual energy.

It is essential to allow uncomfortable sexual feelings from the past to surface and release. Before going to sleep, think about fears regarding difficult sexual situations. Ask your Dream Lover to help release these negative feelings. Tonight is an opportunity to empty out the "sexual garbage" (repressed sexual energy) from the past.

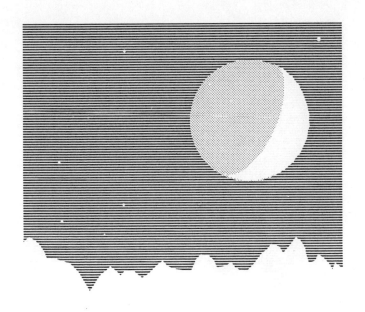

In faith, I open to my sensuousness.

Sensuousness is a key to expressing your
sexuality. Allow yourself to feel sensuous
during your waking hours. It is safe to feel these
sensations. Sensuality can be a gentle
introduction to more intimate moments. This
night, know there is safety in being sensuous.
You have the freedom to do this tonight.

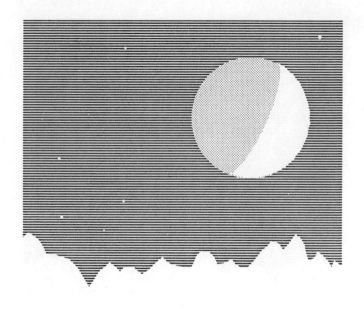

In love's magic I weave the tapestry of intimacy.

Open your heart to love, as you begin to love and appreciate yourself you will, in turn, receive love from others. The intimacy that you express will come back to you. Be assured that the magic of love grows in your dreams and intimacy blossoms like the waxing moon.

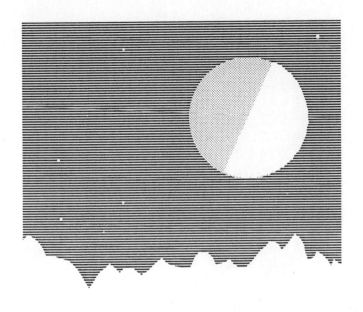

This night, with my dream lover, I feel the stirrings of passion.

Passion can be the vehicle for the energy of your life force energy. By not allowing yourself to express passion, you are not living your life to its full potential. Tonight your Dream Lover guides you through that gateway to self-discovery. Feel passion in your being. Connect with the vibrancy of all living things. Ask Spirit to let the connection of passion and power be within you.

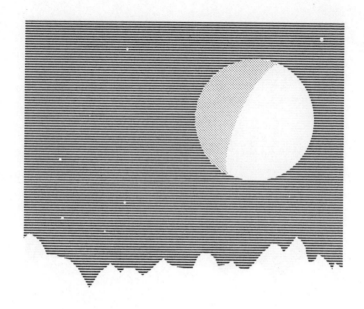

Love flows easily...to me and through me.

By clearing the blocks from the past and allowing your feelings to be your friends, you open yourself to universal love. This means being kind to yourself and finding a special place inside that allows you to feel peace and connection to spirit. Anger, fear, frustration and judgement are the emotions that hold back the flow of love. This night, with your Dream Lover, feel the tide of love wash to you and through you. Awaken with a light heart.

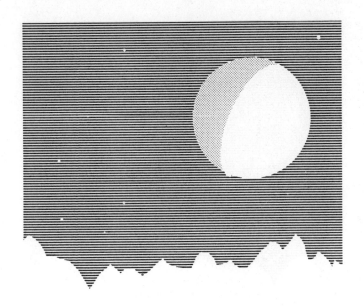

*On this night my dream lover and I will bathe
ourselves in moonbeams of ecstasy.*

Embrace your Dream Lover tonight with the
intention of experiencing ecstasy. Transport
yourself to a place of sheer joy and rapture. Let
these blissful sensations flow into your day.
Take time to relish in the warm sunlight or feel
elated listening to a piece of classical music.
Whatever you do, connect with a feeling of
ecstasy. Nurture and develop ecstasy.
Remember when you see the new moon, it is
reminding you to feel the jubilation of new
beginnings.

My dream love making helps me synchronize with the the rhythm of the tides and the pulse of the planet.

In merging with a dream lover, be aware of your close connection with Mother Earth. Your union is the expression of the God-Force. When two energies coincide there is fusion. The sexual energies that are generated become transformed into positive life force. This life force, in turn, infuses us with more sexual energy and so the energy wheel turns. Tonight your Dream Lover contributes to aligning you with the rhythm of all life.

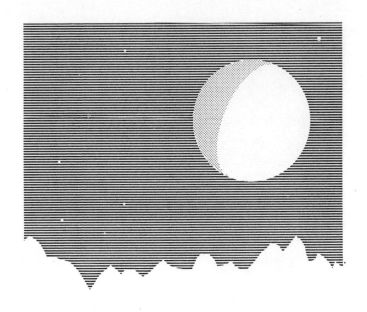

My heart radiates love, compassion and trust
throughout the Universe.

This process is known as falling in love. When your heart is open, love channels through you and to you. The qualities of trust and compassion that you exhibit are reflected in the people around you. When you develop openness of heart you help change the environment around you. The effect is contagious. Ask this night to experience unconditional love.

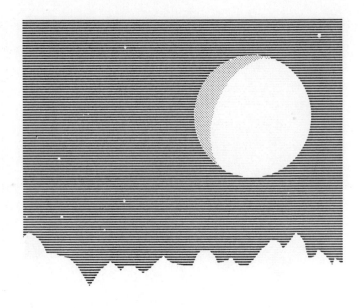

My body is a divine temple that expresses beauty and passion and my Dream Lover pays homage at my temple.

Acknowledge your own grace. When you recognize beauty in yourself then you are able to truly see the beauty in others. Respect and care for your body; the more attention and love you can give yourself, the more pleasure will be returned. Have an intention to become the "best of friends" with your body.

By loving myself more and more everyday, I see the changes that are taking place within my body and within my world.

Your body reflects your subconscious beliefs about yourself and your form is a manifestation of those thoughts. By pledging to love and support yourself, more and more each day, you will become aware of positive physical changes taking place. If you desire to be healthier, more vital and vibrant spend time re-programming negative beliefs you have about your body. Request tonight that your Dream Lover help change the negative concepts that you have about yourself. Delve into the depths of the subconscious mind and change your mind about your body !

I communicate my deepest desires and all my desires are fulfilled. Self-expression comes easily to me.

During your night-time adventures ask that your deepest desires be fulfilled. This means open communication. Using the safe space of being with a Dream Lover, ask for exactly what you desire. By asking directly, clearly and honestly your needs will be met. Your words become law in the universe.

I fully rejoice in my sexuality!

On this night ask your Dream Lover to help you celebrate your sexuality . Should you be feeling afraid or confused, understand that your ego mind has been conditioned to suppress the natural feelings of joy regarding sexuality. It is perfectly acceptable to feel and enjoy your sexual feelings.   Push the ego mind aside and relish your sensuality.

In our sexual encounters, my Dream Lover helps me catapult myself beyond the boundaries of my imagination.

Do not set limitations on your desires. Allow yourself to be taken to the extremes of arousal by your dream lover. Such sensations are powerful. Allowing this life force to permeate every cell of your body, thus revitalizing and regenerating your body. Know you are entitled to experience ecstasy. Go for it!

I yield to divine orgasm with my dream lover. I fully experience all of life.

As your sexual adventures reach the point of orgasm, you are uniting physical, emotional and spiritual energies. Reaching this pinnacle means that you have opened yourself to trust and certainty. You embrace life with open arms, unconditionally.

Tonight my Dream Lover and I float with the clouds.
Warm sunbeams of light dance over our bodies
filling us with perfect joy.

Program yourself to connect with your Dream
Lover by astral travelling to a faraway romantic
place. May you experience sheer bliss and
rapture and fly to the edges of the universe. This
night explore the universe with the one who
wants only to be with you. Let your
imagination soar.

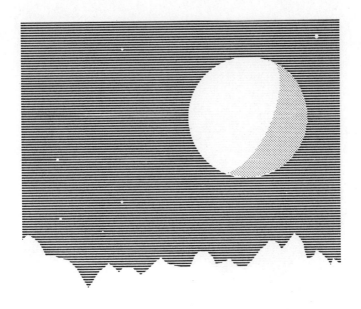

I am willing to accept love. I surrender and flow in unison with my higher self for my highest good.

The minute that we stop resisting is the moment we achieve harmony with our higher self. In being willing to accept love and to surrender to our feelings, we are able to free our spirits to align with the Universal God Force. Accept the gift of love in all forms, i.e. the animal and plant kingdom. Nature is love personified. Accepting love is accepting the Universe around you. Whatever Dream Lover you pull to yourself, love that form and know that it is the perfect teacher for you at that time.

*I am letting go of the struggle within relationships. I
create a perfect loving partner.*

It is important to release pain from all
unresolved relationships. Unsettled
relationships can drain your vital energy and
deaden desire. Go into the past and clear away
those deep hurts. Unresolved problems
connected to your parents will appear in
behavioral patterns manifested in your present
relationships. Your Dream Lover may appear
in your dreams as your mother or father,
perhaps as a way to heal unresolved hurts.
Know that you are, right now, creating loving
relationships.

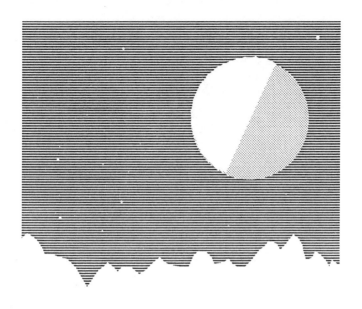

*My relationship with my Dream Lover provides me
with valuable lessons to assist my waking life.*

Invariably each Dream Lover will assist you to
resolve difficulties in your life. Tonight let your
Dream Lover be very clear in bringing you a
message that will affect your well being and
bring you closer to wholeness. Look forward to
inner learning. Ask for guidance that you may
fully understand the messages your dreams
contain.

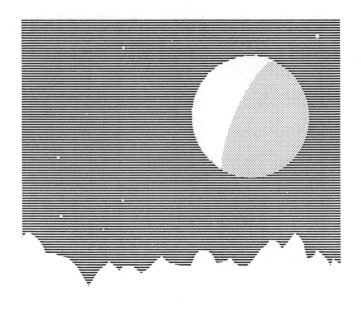

I am able to be wholly at peace. I have nothing to fear.

Tonight let your Dream Lover take you by the hand and direct you to some place you have feared to go alone. Because you trust, you can face that hidden aspect of yourself that you've avoided and let light into every corner. Your inner guidance is leading you to peace.

This night my Dream Lover helps me create the perfect balance of both my male and female energies.

Within each of us, both a feminine and a masculine energy exist. The closer the equilibrium of these co-existing energies, the more in balance we feel. Tonight you integrate the inner male and the inner female and that energy flows freely in dreams. You are loving and accepting of all parts of yourself.

This night I connect with my higher self through my Dream Lover and I am healed.

Visualize your Dream Lover as a channel pouring into you the healing energy from the Universe. You can direct this energy to another or focus on a part of your body or your mind you want to heal. Tonight is a night of healing.

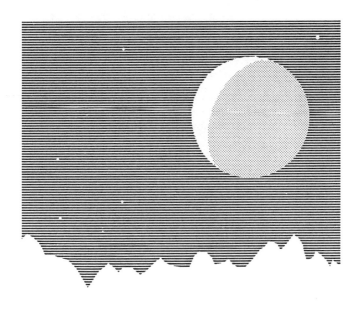

Tonight the power of creativity surges through every pore of my being.

By joining with your Dream Lover you open your root chakra (the first chakra that dwells at the base of the spine) and allow your creative energies to flow. The potency of your creativity is then released and surges through your entire body. Visualize a flame of creativity at the base of your first chakra. As you see the flame get brighter, it moves up your spine and clears blocks that have kept you from your full creative potential. Your Dream Lovers help you increase your creative energy.

In union with my dream lover, I manifest all my
dreams and desires. Miracles flow into my life.

As the male and female aspects of ourselves are
balanced we become more whole and integrated.
Energy is not wasted suppressing that part of
ourself we have not been accepting. This
produces a clear, unified energy within, which
can be focused on manifesting a new glowing
strength. Knowing and believing in that new
strength adds to our ability to create and
manifest our dreams and desires. The union
with your Dream Lover frees you to be all you
desire to be.

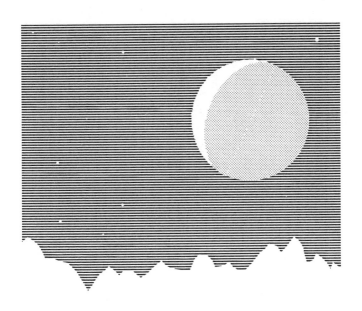

My child within delights and receives, in innocence,
the love of my Dream Lover.

The child within us needs to be loved and
nurtured. Pure delight and playfulness are
qualities naturally expressed by children.
Your Dream Lover tryst can manifest aspects of
the child. Focus on what your child-self is
saying to you. Let the inner child out tonight.
Experience the wonder and expectancy. Be
ready for fun. Expect to be loved.

My Dream Lover is the key to my higher self. I know
that whatever happens to me is all part
of the perfect plan.

Who I am is always safe and at peace. Even
when my life doesn't fit my expectations, I have
trust and faith that my life is unfolding
according to a greater plan. Tonight in my
dreams I know my life is divinely guided and I
am safe.

WHAT DO YOUR DREAM LOVERS MEAN?

As you develop the ability to acquire Dream Lovers you will be aware that all Dream Lovers are not the same. Different types will come at different times in your life to bring a balance. You will, most likely, want to understand what each Dream Lover means and will want to know what area of your life is being balanced by each dream. I've developed an easy method for you to be able to discern what your Dream Lovers are trying to tell you about your life. To understand this system it is valuable to understand the chakra system and the colors or vibratory rates associated with the charkas. Chakras are the invisible but very real energy centers in the body. Although there are thousands of energy centers throughout the body, (the Chinese meridian system details many of them) there are seven very important chakras in the body which lie along a continuum from the base of the spine to the crown of the head.

Each individualized chakra has a particular vibratory rate or manifestation which is attuned to a different ray of life force or a different aspect of your personality. Although colors are traditionally associated with these chakras they are astral colors rather than colors that you can see with the naked eye. If the chakras are open and functioning properly, allowing the full potential of life force energy to flow through them, an individual feels balanced and strong in all areas of life. If one or more of the chakras are closed, an individual will not feel in harmony. Each lover that comes into your dreams will primarily be associated with one chakra more than the others. The energy associated with each chakra can be called a ray. For example the first chakra, which is centered around the genitals, is associated with the Red Ray and represents the qualities of the vibration of the color red. Dream Lovers will not necessarily wear the colors of the ray with which they are associated, but they <u>will</u> be aligned to that color ray and related chakra. As you become aware of the ray your Dream Lover is aligned to, you will be aware of the area within yourself that is being balanced. Each Dream Lover will be primarily balancing a different chakra or energy center of your body. The chakras have all been traditionally correlated to different colors.

There is no doubt that color plays an important role in everyone's life. Using color and chakras to understand your dreams has been used successfully in many cultures with an esoteric tradition. To understand color is to understand the essence of energy. We are living in an expansive ocean of energy consisting of vitally-alive vibrations with different speeds and varying degrees of intensity. This is an ocean of energy that is a swirling dance of ever-changing matter. It is energy in the various stages of solid, liquid and gas each finding its temporary niche in the universe. Light and color are vibrations in this eternal play of energy. The warm colors of red, orange and yellow have a much lower vibratory rate on the electromagnetic scale while the cooler colors of green, blue and purple have a much faster rate.

You are a series of energy fields. Your entire body is constantly vibrating in fields of energy, some subtle and some manifest. You are perpetually involved in movement and motion. Your body's energy fields are affected by the ever-changing energies in your environment such as sunlight and wind, the energy fields of other people and the energy of the food that you take in. Continuously, your body is being deeply affected by the energy of the various color rays.

Dr. Max Luscher, a scientist doing research in how color affects us, explains, "After hundreds of thousands of color tests given in the United States, Europe, Africa, Japan and Australia, we know that every specific color inspires the same stimulus in every single individual no matter what that person's culture may be. Orange-red has a stimulating effect on everyone. Dark blue has a relaxing effect on everyone. Therein lies the universal validity of color psychology. Just as music inspires feeling, renders mood and expresses the very subtlest emotions, so do colors. The hue, degree of lightness and intensity arouse the very same specific sensations in every individual."

Each color is intimately connected with a specific chakra. The lover that appears in your dream **will not necessarily be clothed in the color of the ray with which they are associated,** however he or she will be vibrating with the same qualities with which that ray is associated. He or she will offer the same healing and balancing attributes of that color. Your dream might have a predominance of the color of the ray associated with your dream but this is not usual. Some of this information regarding the different Color Rays was printed in my first book, *Pocketful of Dreams*, but I felt it needed repeating in view of the different Dream Lovers that you will most likely encounter. To understand what part of your life is being balanced, decide what ray or chakra your lover is associated with and then read the section about that ray.

RED RAY LOVERS

Description

The Red Ray Lover corresponds to the first chakra, the area at the base of the spine. More specifically this chakra is located where the sacrum joins the coccyx all the way to the pubic bone in front. Our drive for existence and survival is represented by red. This ray stimulates the physical body to respond and act in an assertive manner. It stimulates the heart and increases the vibratory rate and has a stimulating effect on the appetite.

This first chakra is associated with our basic sexual energy. It is the center of our physical healing and groundedness. It can be related to anger. It is a sign of direct action and active employment. It relates to will and power. Strength, courage, steadfastness, health and vigor are all attributes closely associated with this root chakra.

If the First Chakra is Blocked:

When the first chakra is blocked there is a fear of being in the world and a lack of confidence, self-acceptance and vitality. In addition when this chakra is blocked legs are crossed sometimes even while standing and there is a tendency to put things on the lap.

Physical Characteristics of the Red Ray Lover

The Male Red Ray Lover tends to have a squared-off body with broad shoulders and a square face. He will have thick thighs, and will be well developed. He is full, robust, adventurous, daring and hearty. He wants to make love NOW! He is immediate and enjoys physical sensation. The Female Red Ray Lover is buxom with ripe full breasts and child-bearing hips. She is voluptuous and luscious. She is sensuous and full-mouthed. She shares the qualities of wanting immediate satisfaction and having a passionate embrace of life.

What can the Red Ray Lover in your Dream Symbolize or Heal?

A sensual encounter with a Red Ray Lover can be vitalizing and stimulating and can assist you in overcoming inertia, depression, fear or melancholy. He or she can be a great aid to those who are afraid of life and feel like escaping. The Red Ray Lover will help you plant your feet firmly on the earth. If you tend to dwell too much in the future, the Red Ray Lover will root you in the present...in the NOW. He or she will help supply the energy and motivation necessary in reaching and accomplishing goals. They will help you "get the job done." The Red Ray Lover appearing in your dreams will also help balance you physically if you are feeling sluggish or are having circulation or blood-related difficulties, skin rashes or mental stability. They will also come to help you balance any difficulties within the sexual organs.

The Red Ray Lover Synopsis

Inspires: Freedom, determination, honor, will, power, strength, activity, alertness, independence, motivation, initiative, leadership.

Releases: Anger, frustration, confusion, violence, destruction, revenge, rebellion, impulsiveness, impatience.

ORANGE RAY LOVER

Description

The Orange Ray Lover corresponds to the second chakra. This chakra is located a few inches below the belly button. The energy of this area represents our emotions and drive for social acceptance. The orange ray is warm and stimulating but it is lighter and higher in vibration than red, so the energy translates to broader fields in the body. It stimulates less concern with self-survival and more involvement with assisting in group and social functions. The vibration of the color orange is a happy one. It is a funny color used by clowns the world over. This color stimulates optimism, expansiveness and emotional balance. An Orange Ray Lover in a dream relates to emotions, ambition, exploration, business and most importantly, self-acceptance.

Unlike the Red Ray, which is sensual, the Orange Ray is the social ray. It represents optimism, change, striving, self-motivation, enthusiasm and courage. It stimulates the drive to find reality through other people, the drive for companionship. The Red Ray is a passion for self-preservation and self-gratification, while the Orange Ray's concern is more for social preservation. Orange Ray enhances acceptance of your emotions, and the acceptance of your social love. An open second chakra encourages being unafraid to dance and sing and proclaim yourself as a lover of people.

If the Second Chakra is Blocked:

When the second chakra is blocked there is a difficulty in regard to social behavior patterns and often there are family difficulties. There can also be a lack of self-love, self-esteem and self-acceptance. When this area is blocked an individual will often sit with hands or arms covering this part of the body.

Physical Characteristics of Orange Ray Lovers

You will know that your dream lover is an Orange Ray Lover by his or her physical characteristics. The Orange Ray Lover usually has an oval face with large expressive eyes. He or she will usually be equally proportioned and will be slender. The Orange Ray Lover is emotional, feeling, sensitive, perceiving, and can be mercurial. He or she will often be talkative and concerned about how you are feeling.

What Can the Orange Ray Lover Symbolize or Heal?

The Orange Ray Lover will enter your dreams when you are suppressing emotions and need to be feeling and expressing yourself more. Also, the tendency to believe too readily without weighing with skepticism or discrimination can be healed by the Orange Ray Lover. If you have a tendency to be suspicious or mistrusting or have selfish pride or are seeking power, the Orange Ray Lover can assist in creating balance and discrimination. The healing energies of the Orange Ray Lover stimulate inner knowing that we all are one. Any physical imbalance in your body that is created because of suppressed emotion is assisted by the Orange Ray Lover. There is also a balancing of the health organs in the lower abdominal area.

The Orange Ray Lover Synopsis

Inspires: Optimism, courage, victory, confidence, enthusiasm, encouragement, attraction, plenty, kindness, expansion.

Releases: Superiority, mistrust, power-seeking pride, superficiality.

YELLOW RAY LOVER

Description

The Yellow Ray Lover corresponds to the third chakra. The third chakra is located in the area of the solar plexus. The Yellow Ray is the last of the warm, extraverted color rays and represents the intellectual part of us. In a dream the Yellow Ray Lover relates to your intellectual thinking process. The energy of the Yellow Ray stimulates your logical linear thinking processes and relates to the left brain activities. Yellow stimulates the body to respond with mental discrimination, organization, attention to detail, evaluation, active intelligence, discipline, administration, praise, sincerity and harmony. The Yellow Ray gives heightened expression and freedom which translates into joy within a dream.

If the Third Chakra is Blocked

When this area is blocked there is fear and anxiety about the world "out there." You don't get clear "gut feelings." There is insecurity, self doubt and a lack of expression. The body language when this area is blocked can include hands and arms covering this area, elbows on knees and wearing tight belts.

Physical Characteristics of the Yellow Ray Lover

Physically Yellow Ray Lovers tend to be tall and slender. They tend to have long rectangular faces and high foreheads and long graceful fingers. They radiate a quiet and gentle wisdom and compassion. They are highly creative individuals who seek expression in art, literature and music. They are very skilled in the communication arts. These lovers tend to make love at length and tend to articulate and pre-meditate each erotic play. They are also flexible, expressive, eloquent and intensely self-aware individuals who are efficient in planning and organization.

The spontaneous reaction to stimuli, or the love making that is unique to both the Red and Orange Ray Lovers, easily differentiates them from the Yellow Ray Lover. Instead he or she will have a more detached understanding of how events originate; i.e. where they take place, when they will be brought to focus, etc. The Yellow Ray Lover is interested in the larger scope of life. He or she stimulates our need to live in an orderly world while at the same time expressing our individuality and our need to understand where we fit into the scheme of things.

What Can the Yellow Ray Lover Symbolize or Heal?

The Yellow Ray Lover appearing in a dream can have great healing power in the release of fear. Often, when one is fearful, one's stomach knots or feels as if it were going to turn over. A tremendous amount of fear can be locked in the solar plexus region. Frequently, individuals cannot understand the cause of their fears. The fear can even come from fearful past life experiences. The Yellow Ray Lover will appear in a dream to gradually release the tension from the fearful experience centered in the solar plexus. If you are suppressing any fear or if you are in a fearful or trepidatious time in your life, the Yellow Ray Lover can offer a balance. The Yellow Ray Lover is also very healing for times in your life when you are judgmental, critical or verbally aggressive. It is a ray that will stimulate you to be reflective and open to solving the problem. This lets you be flexible and be adaptable to change. When you align with the Yellow Ray, no problem will remain unsolved under the scrutiny of your intellect. Often it is better to change ourselves than to try to change others and the Yellow Ray Lover will offer a balance between your head and your heart.

The Yellow Ray Lover Synopsis

Inspires: Joy, expression, ability, mental discrimination, organization, attention to detail, evaluation, active intelligence, discipline, administration.

Releases: Self-doubt, possessiveness, jealously, selfish attachment, envy, insecurity, mistrust.

THE GREEN RAY LOVER

Description

The Green Ray Lover in your dreams corresponds to the heart chakra, the fourth energy point between the warm extraverted spectrum of red, orange, and yellow and the cool introverted colors of blue and purple.The Green Ray stimulates feelings of love, balance, harmony, peace, brotherhood, hope, growth and healing. I find often when my clients are healing that they tend to have Green Ray Lovers and the color green will be prominent in their dreams. Green is found everywhere in nature symbolizing the abundant, replenishing forces of the universe. There will always be enough.

If the Fourth Chakra is Blocked

A blockage in this area means lacking trust in

others and a lack of emotional security. It means being afraid to let other people in and it means protecting self because of hurt from the past. When this area is blocked the body language will include holding books or objects tightly over the chest or arms folded across the chest.

Physical Characteristics of Green Ray Lovers

The Green Ray Lover physically tends to have a heart shaped face and be of average height. The most obvious characteristics of these lovers is not their physical appearance so much as their enormous capacity to love. When they appear in a dream, you are aware of an opening of the heart and an expansion of your capacity to be loved and to love.

What Can the Green Ray Lover Symbolize or Heal in a Dream?

These lovers will appear at times when there is a need to expand your heart connection for yourself and others. They will help you become more generous, vital, open-hearted and nurturing. They will also establish an inner security and certainty. When your heart is open you can feel the love of the universe streaming through your being, you feel the greatest security and self-confidence. You learn to live without attachments (the sense of a necessity to hold on to something) and with less attachment to your possessions. The Green Ray Lover is a powerful healer of any physical difficulty throughout the entire body because love is the greatest healer.

The Green Ray Lover Synopsis

Inspires: Encouragement, abundance, generosity, vitality, power, security, open-heartedness, nurturing, self-assertion, compassion, expansion, sharing, harmony, balance.

Releases: Self-doubt, possessiveness, jealousy, selfish attachment, envy, insecurity, mistrust.

THE BLUE RAY LOVER

Description

The Blue Ray Lover is associated with the throat chakra. The Blue Ray is the first of the cool spectrum colors. It stimulates you to seek inner truth. When the Blue Ray Lover appears in your dreams, he or she is there to help you to attain inner peace, mental security and to live in harmony with your ideals. They stimulate your spiritual security and desire for inner understanding.

If the Fifth Chakra is Blocked

When the throat chakra is blocked there is a stifling of creativity and self-expression. A blockage usually means very frustrated communication and a lack of ability to compromise.

Physical Description of the Blue Ray Lover

The Blue Ray Lovers are usually smooth-skinned and tall. They will have a lofty, if not aloof, presence and yet radiate a lovely peaceful mien. They tend to have long oval faces rather than the square face of the Red Ray Lover or the heart-shaped face of the Green Ray Lover. They are apt to be idealistic, patient and enduring souls. They make very patient lovers. And your love making is likely to be long, slow and very peaceful. These lovers tend to be nostalgic, committed, devotional, peaceful and loyal in nature. These highly sensitive individuals live in a mental world colored by their own commitment to idealistic concepts and feelings. They seek contentment and peace of mind.

What Can a Blue Ray Lover Symbolize or Heal?

A Blue Ray Lover will enter your dreams to stimulate peace, inspiration, spiritual understanding, faith and devotion. If you are in need of gentleness, contentment, patience and composure, the Blue Ray Lover will enter your dreams. The Blue Ray is also beneficial for someone who acts compulsively without stopping to think. This lover can be extremely liberating for those who have become rigid and resistant to change. The true blue of sincerity manifests in all relationships in life and the Blue Ray Lover can come to aid you in gaining sincerity and peace within all your relationships.

The Blue Ray Lover Synopsis

Inspires: Love, wisdom, gentleness, trust, understanding, detachment, kindness, compassion, patience, forgiveness, sensitivity, contemplation.

Releases: Self-pity, fear, self-rejection, separateness, isolation, worry, depression, passivity, anxiety, coldness, detachment.

THE PURPLE RAY LOVER

Description

The Purple Ray Lover relates to the brow chakra, your intuition, and is the color most deeply associated with dreams. Listen carefully to those dreams where the Purple Ray Lover steps forward. This lover will stimulate your ability to be one with the universe, to have conflict-free relationships and to put yourself out in front in the realm of human development. As with the Blue Ray Lover, the effects are calming, soothing, and comforting. Record and contemplate these dreams, for the dreams of the Purple Ray Lover will most likely give you insight into your deepest inner self and the world around you.

Moving through the different rays and the Dream Lovers associated with each Ray, it is interesting to note what happens to our vision of time. The closer we are to our senses, the more time seems to flow forward. The closer we are to our imagination, the more time seems to flow in all directions. When the Red Ray Lover comes into our dreams, we receive a vision of the immediate "now," like the cat eyeing a mouse. When we view the present with our intellect (yellow ray) we get a vision of logic like the flow of traffic on a freeway. When we perceive with our feeling (blue) we receive a vision of history like rings on a tree. When we view reality with our intuition (purple), we get a vision of the future like an eagle soaring high above the plains and looking down. From that vantage point one can see what is near but also what is beyond. Therefore, when you have a Purple Ray Dream Lover you are perceiving beyond. These dreams will tend to be clothed in prophecy, the dreams of a visionary.

If the Sixth Chakra is Blocked

A blockage will mean that there is a lack of ability to gain access to intuition. Telepathy and inner vision will be blocked.

Physical Characteristics of the Purple Ray Lover

Physically the Purple Ray Lovers tend to be illusive and lovemaking is not so much physical as it is a communion or a uniting of spirit. Often there is no memory of a visible or physical presence. Rather they are often just wisps of dreams from which you awake refreshed and renewed with spiritual clarity and intuitive knowing.

What Can the Purple Ray Lover Symbolize or Heal?

The Purple Ray Lovers will enter your dreams when you are needing to step out of your mind and into your intuition. They will come in times of spiritual uncertainty to assist you in finding clarity.

The Purple Ray Lover Synopsis

Inspires: Inspiration, vision, far-sightedness, trust in the future, tuning into the inner worlds of others, supersensitivity.

Releases: Inability to live in the now, spacing out, forgetfulness, lack of discipline, resentment, separateness, arrogance, pride, contempt.

THE WHITE RAY DREAM LOVER

Description

This lover in your dreams corresponds to your crown chakra at the top of your head. This ray is the fastest and the most frequent of the color spectrum. These lovers have the effect on our being of divine realization, humility and creative imagination. They can have a purifying effect like the white snow in wintertime. The White Ray encompasses all colors. These are also very special and important dreams. When these lovers come into your dreams they have the energy and power to transform the focus of the imagination.

If the Seventh Chakra is Blocked

A blockage here can contribute to feeling alone and not at-one with all of life. There is a lack of unity with all things. Life seems separate and not connected.

Physical Characteristics of the White Ray Lover

Like the Purple Ray Lover, often the White Ray Lover doesn't seem to have a physical body. They can appear as a light or a feeling or as a radiant light being. These dream love encounters are usually etheric and even life transforming.

These are dreams to watch and remember.

What Can the White Ray Lover Symbolize or Heal?

These dreams will come to lead you to higher spiritual attunement and divine love. They will increase your sense of wonder, bliss and self-surrender. These love encounters can be a great healing for a person with a negative self-image for they hold the power of transformation.

The White Dream Lover Synopsis

Inspires: Mystical instinct, creativity, spirit-inspiration, meditation, reflection, deep inner wisdom, grace, delight, spiritual unity.

Releases: Obsessiveness, martyrdom, restriction, intolerance, day-dreaminess, pessimism.

Every now and then you might have what I call the 'Rainbow Lover'. Those individuals who have experimented with Dream Lovers declare that these are the best lovers of all for these lovers encompass all the rays. The experience with a Rainbow Lover can seem almost like merging so totally that there is no separation between the two of you. You become one self.

USING CRYSTALS TO ATTAIN A
DREAM LOVER

The stones that are discussed here are a few that may be used to assist you is discovering your dream lovers. It's important to remember that, of themselves, these stones can do nothing. It is your intention that activates them for dream use.

Crystals

Crystals have been used since the beginning of time as objects of wonder and as a means of understanding and viewing unseen worlds. Their mystique spans time and culture alike. They are an excellent stone to use for any Dream Lover work that you do!!!

Crystals are basically magnifiers and transmitters. They are used in radios. In fact, silicon, which is in the crystal family, is the basis of computer technology. It allows for the processing of enormous amounts of information by transmitting electrical current over its crystalline structure. As there is a bio-electrical current within human beings, we can literally avail ourselves of the power of crystals to "transmit" or enhance dream states by transmitting our intention through its crystalline structure.

To utilize crystal for gaining a dream lover:

1. The right crystal - Obtain a rock crystal that "speaks" to you. This means you intuitively know that this crystal is for you and your dreams. It is preferable to have a crystal that is used just for dream lovers and nothing else.

2. Cleansing - The best way to cleanse a crystal (or any stone) dedicated to dreams is to leave the crystal outdoors on a clear night when there is a full moon. Place the stone so that the moonlight may shine directly on it all night. If that is not possible, you can:

   a. Rub your crystal with eucalyptus oil.
   b. Let your crystal soak in water and sea salt.
   c. Place your crystal outdoors in sunlight for at least five hours.
   d. Place in the ocean or a running clear stream for an hour.

3. Dedicating the crystal - To dedicate your crystal (or any stone), hold it up to your third eye and say a dedication, either quietly or aloud. Program your crystal for only one thing at a time. Some sample dedications are:

"I dedicate you, Dream Crystal, to dream love experiences that allow my spirit to soar so that my waking life is more joyous."

"I dedicate you, Dream Crystal, to Dream Lovers that empower me with a positive vision of myself and a strong belief in my own self-worth."

"I dedicate you, Dream Crystal, to Dream Lovers that will enable me to develop my own unique creative skills".

"I dedicate you, Dream Crystal, to Dream Lovers that will allow my relationships with men and women to heal."

"I dedicate you, Dream Crystal, to Dream Lovers that will give me powerful insights into my future."

"I dedicate you, Dream Crystal, to Dream Lovers that will assist in the healing of myself and others."

"I dedicate you, Dream Crystal, to Dream Lovers that will deepen my connection with Spirit and God."

It is not necessary to dedicate each night. However, if you are going to change your intentions, cleanse and re-dedicate it.

4. Dream Door - Put your Dream Crystal in a special place when you are not using it. You can put it in black silk to hold the energy or you can place it in a special location where you can admire it during the day.

At night, place it near your sleeping area. Just before sleep, hold the crystal to your third eye and imagine that your consciousness is melting into its fluid light structure. Imagine that within this shimmering orb of moon-satin light is a Mystical Door to your dreams. See that door opening. Know that you have opened the mysterious door to your inner realms. Then keep your crystal near you during the night.

Amethyst

Amethyst is also in the crystal family. Its rich purple reflects the ability to move easily from one reality to another. The color associated with the third eye is purple and this magical stone can be used to open the third eye area to gain spiritual dream lovers. It is a calming and emotionally balancing stone. As it calms the mind and emotions, our innermost nature can come forth in our dreams.

Moonstone

The moonstone is an excellent stone to help gain a dream lover. This stone with its moonlike, silvery-white light undulating on its surface, is sacred in India. It is used as a gift for lovers and is believed to arouse tender passion and give lovers the ability to see into the future. In many cultures it is felt that this stone changes with the phases of the moon. As the cycles of the moon are connected to dream cycles, the moonstone connects us more deeply with our inner dream states.

Moonstone is also soothing to the emotions. It is a good stone to program for very loving heart-connected dreams. You will obtain the most loving dream lovers with this stone. Keep the moonstone near you while you sleep or tape a small one on your third eye area.

Selenite

This very translucent crystal is ruled by the moon. It is named for Selene, the Greek goddess of the moon. A very powerful stone is used to gain understanding of one's personal truth through a dream lover. It can allow for a deep calming and the attainment of profound inner states. It symbolizes pure spirit and can be used for spiritual advancement. Selenite is also an alchemic key to past life lovers and future life lovers.

Selenite is aligned to your crown chakra and is a powerful tool for developing intuition and telepathic powers through your dream lovers. Use it for stimulating dreams of mental and spiritual clarity. It also can be an excellent stone for telepathic communication during the night so it is excellent to use for dream sharing.

Pearls

Pearls, though not technically stones, are excellent to use in regard to dreams. These silvery orbs from the sea are ruled by the moon. They originate from the oyster, a living species found in the sea. Not only does the moon affect the tides and the creatures of the sea, she also greatly affects our dream states. The very formation of the pearl is conducive to dream states. The layers are deposited in a concentric manner. The spherical shape, the soft luminescent color and the multi-layers are all symbolic of the non-linear nature of dreams. The concentric fashion in which they weave through our consciousness symbolizes the dream state. Pearls come from the sea and, even upon land, maintain their connection to the fluidity, the ebbing and flowing, and the intuitive nature of water and the sea.

Pearls from the ocean are more potent for dreams

than are freshwater pearls because salt water is a better conductor of electrical energy. The fact that saltwater pearls originate in the ocean means they are eternally connected with the sea. That alignment allows for a better intuitive connection with your bio-electrical flows. The greater the bio-electrical flow in your body, the more intense and vivid your dreams will be. Having pearls in your dream space will assist in experiencing Dream Lovers that will increase your intuitive nature.

Dream Pillows

One way to enhance your probability of a Dream Lover is to make a dream pillow filled with special herbs. It remains unknown whether or not there is some special ingredient within these herbs that facilitates dreams, or whether it is a behavioral response connecting your dream desire to the aroma. Because the dream pillow is with you for the duration of your sleeping hours, it acts as a constant subliminal reminder of your intention to connect with a Dream Lover.. For obtaining a Dream Lover, I suggest that you make a dream pillow filled with lavender. Smelling it while sleeping is not only thought to assist you in remembering your dreams, but it also establishes a connection between the fragrance of the herbs and your desire for a special dream. Using a dream pillow really works.

The best way to prepare a dream pillow is to:

1. Make sure that the herbs are of the highest quality and optimally pesticide-free.

2. Use a natural fiber when making the pillowcase. The very best fabric to use is silk as this is an excellent conductor of bio-electrical energy. Wool is also excellent. Many meditators and yogis meditate on wool or sheepskin because this helps them align with the bio-electrical energy flows of the planet. Using wool or silk for your dream pillow will allow you to experience dreams that are more potent because you will be more bio-electrically balanced.

I suggest using lavender or purple-colored material because these are the colors of the portal to dreams and they will contribute to the power of your dream pillow.

3. Use your dream pillow only at night for dreams so that is the only thing you associate with it. You might keep it in a special box or covering and only take it out at night for dreaming. The fragrance will then be an intimate reminder of the alignment between you and your dreams.

4. Hold the pillow close to your nose as you drift off to sleep. Keep uppermost in your thoughts the desire for a dream. In the morning, deeply inhale the fragrance of your dream pillow. Very often this will revive the memory of a dream.

5. Pat Nugent's Dream Pillow is made in the heart shape and has all the ribbons of the rainbow on it. When she desires a Yellow Ray Dream Lover she ties a knot in the yellow ribbon before bed. Or if she desires a Red Ray Lover (Red Ray Lovers have a high rating with her!!!) she ties a knot in the red ribbon before bed.

DEDICATING YOUR DREAM LOVER EXPERIENCES

Before bed you can dedicate the energy of your night hours. You can dedicate your dreams to the health of your children or to world peace or to your own physical healing. Know that as you dream you are creating energy and that energy has an empowering effect on you and the world around you. Where intention goes energy flows. Intend that the energy generated by your dreams is dedicated to your highest good and so it will be.

I've just finished writing this book. The hour is late and the city is being softly blanketed in snow. I've started to think about all that I've written about dream lovers . Reading it over, it sounds easy. Just like my bookcase that came in the box with "easy to follow instructions". This was the same bookcase that ended up as firewood after two weeks of trying to assemble the "easy-to-assemble" shelves. And I'm reminded of the oven cleaner commercial where the homemaker, in high heels, waltzes out into the kitchen, opens the oven.. sprays...wipes ...smiles and says.."It's easy!"

Come on! When have you ever cleaned an oven...and it was easy?

Actually, obtaining dream lovers <u>can</u> be easy. Honest! Sometimes it just happens! But it can also take practice and perseverance. If you've read this book, faithfully done the exercises, but still feel like the 'Nerd of the Nocturnal Set' because you get cabbages and back doors and wash tubs in your dreams...but never...not even once... a Dream Lover. Take heart!

Often a Dream Lover will appear after you've given up hope of ever having a romantic dream dalliance. But until that time you can create a Day Dream Lover. A Day Dream Lover can offer all the juiciness and fun of a Dream Lover. To create a Day Dream Lover, let your imagination flow. Imagine that you are having joyous, wondrous loving experiences. Day Dream!!! Your impossible dreams can become a reality.

As we journey through time and space, approaching a new millennium, our dreams will become increasingly important. They will offer guidance and inspiration. They will be as beacons of light on the darkest night. They will allow us to touch the deepest recesses of our soul. In the years ahead, may your Dream Lover carry you laughing through the midnight skies and dancing through the stars, to the farthest reaches of the universe. Sweet Dreams!!!

PAST LIVES PRESENT DREAMS

A complete pocket handbook described by many as one of the most creative works on the connection between past lives and dreams. This book is an Australian best seller and is already into its third reprint. Denise has been able to provide simple, straightforward information that is not only a must for a beginner, but also is excellent reference material for the enthusiast.

Topics covered in 'Pocketful of Dreams' include

- Journeys into Past Lives
- Dreams and Past Lives
- Spirit Guides
- Inner Exploration Exercises
- The Next Step

A must for anyone who has ever dreamed!

Other Titles By Denise Linn

POCKETFUL OF DREAMS

Dreams are secret messages from your mind. Dreams are your greatest tool for understanding yourself and your life. However, very few people recognize how to access this free source of inner power, wisdom and guidance. This book provides answers to the most perplexing questions about the mysterious world of dreams.

When you sleep tonight you can:
* Distinguish between a true prophetic dream and a message from your subconscious.
* Remember your dreams and recognise their meaning.
* Use dreaming to tackle any daytime problem and wake with a solution.
* Experience a dream lover.
* Have revealing communication with the most important people in your life.
* Harness the power of dreams to transform your life.
* Heal self, children and loved ones.
* Develop the skill of astral projection.
* Meet your dream guide.
* Interpret dream symbols.
* Create a dream shield.
* Explore past lives.
* Learn to 'call' animals.
* Tap the vast well of creativity within you.
* Overcome your greatest fears.
* Use the moon, the seasons and the hour of the day to assist dream interpretations.

A message from the Publisher

After reading this fascinating book you will probably want to hear and meet Denise Linn in person. Denise regularly conducts seminars on dreams and past lives in almost every English speaking country in the world.

For information about any of her seminars in the Southern Hemisphere write to:

Nacson Promotions International Pty. Ltd.
P.O. Box 515
Brighton-Le-Sands, NSW 2216
Australia

For information in the Northern Hemisphere write to:

Denise Linn Seminars
Suite 120
1463 E Republican Street
Seattle, Washington 98112

Denise Linn is currently researching her fourth book and would be pleased to hear from any reader about their experiences with dreams. Letters should be addressed to one of the above.

Cover design

Concept, design and finished art by Chris Wills , Leon Nacson, Max and Jan Lay, Rhett Nacson, and Eli Nacson.

Arms supplied by Thomas and Meran Tallis.

Final typesetting and layout by Eli Nacson and Joanne Nikolas.

Final editing and proofing by Jenny Moalem.

Cover design

Concept, design and finished art by Chris Wills, Leon Nacson, Max and Jan Lay, Rhett Nacson and Eli Nacson.

Arms supplied by Thomas and Meran Tallis.

This book was written, edited, proofed and printed using a desktop publishing system.

Writing and editing was done on Apple Macintosh 128K, 512K and Plus computers, using MacWrite and Microsoft WORD. Graphics were produced using Superpaint. Final page layout was accomplished using Aldus PageMaker.

Proofing was done using an Apple Imagewriter II printer. Final formatting and printing was done using an Apple Macintosh IIci computer and an Apple Laserwriter II NTX printer.

Body type is Times 13pt, with Times 13pt italic for emphasis. Dream text is set in ITC Zaph Chancery 13pt. Headers are ITC Zaph Chancery 12pt.

Formatting, graphics, final proofing, final printing and computer consulting was provided by Karl Bettinger AOF, of:

ECHO OLYMPIC COMPUTER
SERVICES
Post Office Box 515
Brighton-Le-Sands NSW 2216 Australia
or in the USA
tel (206) 328-9180

Apple, ImageWriter II, LaserWriter II NTX, and MacWrite are trademarks of Apple Computer, Inc, Cupertino, California, USA

Microsoft WORD is a registered trademark of Microsoft Corp., Redmond Washington USA

Aldus PageMaker is a registerd trademark of Aldus Corp., Seattle, Washington USA.

Superpaint is a registered trademark of Silicon Beach Software, Inc. San Diego, California USA

Macintosh is a trademark of McIntosh Laboratories, Inc., USA

Times is a trademark of Allied Corporation, USA

ITC Zapf Chancery is a trademark of International Typeface Corp, USA